The publisher would like to thank the following people for their special help in producing this book: Sue Riley of Main Street Design for her design of the cover and the title page and her creation of the alphabet letters; Paul Galkoski for his layout of the drawings; Pat Lesnefsky for her typing of the text; and our wives, Ethel Longstreet for the help she provided to Stephen, and Jill Schneider for putting up with the publisher. This book was typeset by Axiom Design Systems in New York City, and was printed on acid-free paper by Arcata Graphics in Kingsport, Tennessee. The cover was printed by New England Book Components in Hingham, Massachusetts. My thanks to the many people I worked with at these firms.

STEPHEN LONGSTREET has studied and drawn the jazz scene throughout America and Europe for over sixty years. And he has much to show for his efforts: several histories of the jazz world, including *Storyville to Harlem, The Real Jazz New and Old, Sportin' House: The Birth of Jazz, Sometimes I Wonder: The Story of Hoagy Carmichael,* and *The Complete Dictionary of Jazz*; several one-man shows and an oeuvre of artworks that can be found in collections such as the Oakland Museum, Yale and Boston Universities, the New Orleans Jazz Museum, the Library of Congress, the Smithsonian Institution, and numerous private collections.

But Mr. Longstreet has done much more than document the jazz world in his special way. He is also the author of over twenty-five novels, several of them best-sellers, and of histories ranging from the Indian Wars to Los Angeles. He is the author of the book for the award-winning musical *High Button Shoes,* and the screenplays of such films as *The Jolson Story* and *Stallion Road.* Add a few memoirs and travel books, drawings for *The New Yorker,* film criticism for *The Saturday Review,* and war correspondence for *Time,* and you have a remarkable career that's still going strong.

A native of New Brunswick, New Jersey, Mr. Longstreet is now a resident of Southern California.

*Linda's,* 6715 Melrose Avenue, Santa Monica, 934-6199
*Maxi's Lounge,* 305 Bristol Street, Costa Mesa,
    593-2137
*Myron's Ballroom,* 1224 S. Grant Street, 748-3045
*Nucleus Nuisance,* 7267 Melrose Avenue,
    W. Hollywood, 939-8666
*Palomino,* 6907 Lankershim Boulevard, Pasadena, 818
    764-4011
*Suntan Room,* 4100 Admiralty Way, Marina del Rey,
    301-3000
*Vine Street Grill,* 1610 Vine Street, 463-4375
*Windows on Hollywood,* 1755 N. Highland Avenue,
    462-1881

## NEW ORLEANS

Start with a visit to the New Orleans Jazz Museum. Much of it good background to the jazz men and women, their music, some of the myths and hype. To get the flavor of the old classic jazz, visit some of the joints along Bourbon and Royal Streets, and *Preservation Hall,* 726 St. Peter Street. If you're still jiving, these are a few of the late-night cellars to head for: *The Westwood Club, Hilltop Night Club, The Tiawanna.*

## CHICAGO

*Andy's,* 11 E. Hubbard, North of the Loop, 642-6805

*At the Tracks,* 325 N. Jefferson, West of the Loop, 332-1124

*The Bulls,* 1916 N. Lincoln Park West, Old Town, 337-3000

*Cotton Club,* 1710 S. Michigan Avenue, 341-9787

*Georgia's,* 230 W. Kinzie, 644-2290

*Get Me High Lounge,* 1758 N. Honore, Bucktown, 252-4090

*The Green Mill,* 4802 N. Broadway, 878-5552 (since 1907)

*Pops for Champagne,* 2934 N. Sheffield, DePaul, 472-1000

*Joe Segal's Jazz Showcase,* 636 S. Michigan Avenue, 427-4300

There are also a number of clubs that specialize in the blues, including three in the DePaul district: *B.L.U.E.S.,* 2519 N. Halsted, 528-1012; *Kingston Mines,* 2548 N. Halsted, 477-4646; and *Wise Fools,* 2270 N. Lincoln, 929-1510; as well as *New Checkerboard Lounge,* 423 E. 43rd Street, South Side, 624-3240 and *Biddy Mulligan's,* 7644 N. Sheridan, Rogers Park, 761-6532.

## LOS ANGELES

*Catalina,* 1640 North Cahuenga Boulevard, Hollywood, 466-2210

*Islander's Café,* 3950 Wilshire Boulevard, 389-5742

*Jazz Lounge,* 8440 Sunset Boulevard, West Hollywood, 650-8999

## NIGHT JAZZ—THE CLUBS

**H**ere are some of the best jazz clubs in four of the jazz centers of the United States: New York, Chicago, Los Angeles, and New Orleans. There are phone numbers so that you can call ahead and see what's on. For the New York and Chicago areas, there are numbers you can call to find out the week's jazz events: for New York, the WGBO Jazzline, 718-465-7500; for Chicago, the Jazz Institute's Hotline, 312-666-1881.

### NEW YORK CITY

*Arthur's Tavern,* 57 Grove Street, Greenwich Village, 675-6879

*Birdland,* 2745 Broadway (not the original), Upper West Side, 749-2228

*Blue Note,* 131 W. 3rd Street, Greenwich Village, 475-8592

*Carlos I,* 432 Sixth Avenue, Greenwich Village, 982-3260

*Fat Tuesday's,* 190 Third Avenue, Chelsea, 533-7902

*Fortune Garden Pavilion,* 209 E. 49th Street, Midtown, 753-0101

*Knitting Factory,* 47 E. Houston Street, Greenwich Village, 219-3055

*Sweet Basil,* 88 Seventh Avenue South, Greenwich Village, 242-1785

*Village Gate,* 160 Bleecker Street, Greenwich Village, 475-5120

*Village Vanguard,* 178 Seventh Avenue South, Greenwich Village, 255-4037

a wild night -
including
the artists

IV '51

1353, 91793; Jim Alsover, 714-985-3352. *Westminster,* 13171 Cedar St. 92683; John McCormick, 714-847-0139.

HAWAII: *Honolulu,* Box 22862, 96822; Don Sharp, 808-533-1587.

NEVADA: *Reno,* Box 125, 89504. *Virginia City,* Box 423, 89440, 702-847-0313.

NEW MEXICO: *Rio Grande,* 505-883-5258.

## NORTHWEST

COLORADO: *Boulder,* 954 W. Alder, Louisville 80027; Pete Clemens, 303-665-7990. *Broadmoor,* 1403 Mesa Ave., Colorado Springs 80906; Richard Donahue, 303-635-4690. *Central City,* Box 339, 80427; Alan Granruth, 303-234-4378. *Choice City,* 1229 Teakwood Dr., Fort Collins, 80525; Chuck Patton, 303-484-7336. *Colorado Springs* (Pikes Peak), Box 38352, 80937. *Denver,* 5920 W. Plymouth Dr., Littleton 80123; Vern Baumer, 303-985-1687; **Hotline:** 303-795-8960.

MONTANA: *Montana,* Box 856, Helena 59624; Rita Frankporter, 406-443-4754. *Billings,* Box 23144, 59104, 406-248-6987. *Flathead Valley,* Box 2627, Kalispell 59903; Dick Fazio, 406-755-6275.

OREGON: *Oregon,* Box 7432, Eugene 97401; Norm Gernhardt, 503-747-7725. *Bay Area,* Box 544, Coos Bay 97420; Gloria Owen, 503-756-7796. *Cascades Ragtime,* Box 193, Riddle 97469. *Oregon City,* Box 214, 97045; Alton Smedstad, 503-648-5149. *Southern Oregon,* Box 1001, Ashland 97520; Larry Bernard, 503-779-6149. *Willamette Valley,* Box 307, Albany 97321; Bob French, 503-393-2976.

WASHINGTON: *Grays Harbor,* Box 646, Aberdeen 98520. *Ocean Shores Dixieland,* Box 293, 98569; Harry Thompson, 206-289-2566. *San Juan Island,* Box 1666, Friday Harbor 98250; Connie Erickson, 206-378-2041; **Hotline:** 206-378-5509. *Seattle* (Puget Sound), 19701 11th Ave. N.W., 98177; Rusty Rathfelder, 206-722-7938; **Hotline:** 206-325-2549. *Spokane,* Box 162, 99210; Larry Richards, 509-747-0098. *Tacoma* (Commencement Bay), Box 520, 98401; Shan Edwards, 206-759-9636. *Tri-Cities,* 1016 W. Columbia Dr., Kennewick 99336, 509-586-3185.

## CANADA

BRITISH COLUMBIA: *Chilliwack,* 45966 Yale Rd., V2P 2M3, 604-795-3600. *Vancouver* (Happy Jazz), 1755 Haro St. #1401, V6G 1H2; Witt Mueller, 604-682-2148. *Vancouver* (Hot Jazz), 2120 Main St., V5T 3C5, 604-873-4131.

ONTARIO: *Kitchener* (Golden Triangle), Box 1671, N2G 4R2; Bob Lane, 519-893-7055. *Toronto* (Duke Ellington), 95 Thorncliffe Park Dr., M4H 1L7.

Our thanks to *TJ Today,* Box 533, Watsonsville, CA 95077, 408-728-3948, for collecting this information and helping to keep the spirit alive.

## SOUTHWEST

ARIZONA: *Arizona*, 5927 E. Thomas Rd. Scottsdale 85251; Dick Knutson, 602-990-2202. *Tucson*, Box 44163, Tucson 85733; Tom Ervin, 602-624-4462; **Hotline:** 602-623-2463.

CALIFORNIA (North): *Northern California New Orleans*, Box 27232, San Francisco, 94127, 415-398-JASS; **Hotline:** 415-398-NOJC. *Central California*, Box 3839, Pinedale 93650; Cal Dortello, 209-225-9822. *Central Valley*, Box 3249, Turlock 95381. Chico, Box 4214, 95927. *Citrus Heights* (Sac'a Jazz Nuts), 240 Pau Hana Circle, 95621; Tom Hughes, 916-723-6353. *El Granada* (Bach Dancing & Dynamite), Box 302, 94018, 415-726-4143. *Feather River*, Box 677, Graeagle 96103; Garrett Smith, 916-836-2838. *Fresno Dixieland*, Box 16399, 93755; **Hotline:** 209-292-DXXY. *High Sierra*, Box 712, Three Rivers 93271, 209-561-4418. *Modesto Dixieland*, 333 Fortuna, 95355; Jeannie Wemken, 209-524-3517. *Monterey Bay*, Box 1872, Salinas 93902; Len Williams, 408-372-6293. *Napa Valley*, Box 175, St. Helena 94574; John Heimann, 707-963-0807. *Rivercity*, 1596 Lodgepole Ave., Anderson 96007; Craig Williams. *Sacramento*, Box 15604, 95813, 916-372-3719; **Hotline:** 916-962-2266. *Sacramento Ragtime*, 5600 Omni Dr., Sacramento 95841; Larry Applegate, 916-961-6056. *San Francisco Ragtime*, Box 42453, 94142. *San Joaquin Dixieland*, Box 4746, Stockton 95204; John Hannan, 209-478-6311. *San Jose*, 586 N. First St. #221, 95112. *Santa Rosa* (T.R.A.D.J.A.S.S.), Box 2861; Tom Barnebey, 707-542-3973. *South Bay*, 43019 Grenna Terr., Fremont 94538; George Smith, 415-656-4731.

CALIFORNIA (South): *Southern California*, 1016 W. Santa Cruz St., San Pedro 90731; Jack Widmark, 213-547-0965. *Southern California New Orleans*, Box 15212, Long Beach 90815; John Anderson, 714-544-8414. *Central Coast*, Box 1193, San Luis Obispo 93406; Betty Brown, 805-543-6404. *Channel Cities*, Box 3738, Ventura 93006; Mike Salmons, 805-644-1838. *Del Mar*, Box 2917, 92014, 619-481-3005. *Desert Dixieland*, Box 1000, Cathedral City 92234, 619-321-JASS. *Encino* (Poor Angel), 5719 Bertrand Ave., 91316; Bob Taber, 213-343-2834. *Inland Empire North*, Riverside, 714-683-0370. *Inland Empire South*, Moreno Valley, 714-663-4467. *Lake Elsinore;* John Sheppard, 714-678-5522. *Los Angeles* (Jazz Forum), Box 65-231, 90065, 213-256-5825. *San Diego* (Dixieland), Box 82776, 92138, 619-297-JASS. *Santa Clarita Dixieland*, Box 2331, Canyon Country 91351; Barbara McGee, 805-949-1449. *Santa Paula*, 117 W. Virginia Terr., 39060. *Simi Valley*, 7131 Owensmouth Ave #103B, Canoga Park 91303; Bill Roberts, 818-349-2448. *South Bay New Orleans*, 4340 1/2 W. 102 St., Inglewood; Max Strehler, 213-378-3182. *Southeast Dixieland*, Box 1012, Commerce 90091; Ray Lyon, 213-927-5966. *Valley Dixieland*, 5658 Winnetka Ave., Woodland Hills 91367; Gus Willmorth, 213-883-4562. *Ventura Big Band*, Box 3738, 90336; Randolph Siple, 805-644-1838. *West Covina Dixieland*, Box

TEXAS: *Dallas,* Box 35023, 75235; Dale McFarland, 915-827-9467. *El Paso,* 8101 Magnetic, 79904; Bob Foskett, 915-751-2878. *Kerrville* (New Orleans Club), Box 1225, 78028; Bill Bacin, 512-896-2285. *Midland,* Box 3790, 79702; Max Christensen, 915-682-5334.

VIRGINIA: *Charlottesville* (Hall of Fame), Box 3210 University Sta., 22903. *Goose Creek,* Welbourne, Middleburg; Nathaniel Morison, 703-687-6035. *Northern Va. Ragtime,* Box 494, Manassas 22110, 703-791-3063.

## MIDWEST

ILLINOIS: *Chicago* (Jazz Institute), Box 7231, 60680, 312-664-4069; **Hotline:** 312-666-1881. *Chicago* (Royal Gardens), 410 S. Michigan Ave., #469, 60605; Dean Peaks, 312-975-9471. *Mundelein* (Good Time), Box 577, 60060; Jim Wallace, 312-566-7333.

INDIANA: *Illiana,* Box 57, Hammond 46325; Eddy Banjura, 312-755-8312. *Indianapolis,* Box 44312, 46204; Steven Holzer, 317-299-0561.

IOWA: *Davenport* (Bix Beiderbecke), 904 W. 14th St., 52804. - *Sturgis Falls Dixieland,* 28 River Ridge La., Cedar Falls 50613, 319-266-1741. *Tri-State,* Box 515, Burlington 52601; Ralph Drish, 319-367-5252.

KANSAS: *Kansas City,* 360 Terrace Trl. W., 66106; Dick Rippey, 913-649-9510; **Hotline:** 816-333-2227. *Topeka,* Box 452, 66601; Jim Monroe, 913-273-0186.

MICHIGAN: *West Michigan,* Box 4290, Muskegon 49444; Jack Robinson, 616-676-1320. West Shore, Box 4177, Muskegon 49444; Victor Blakeman, 616-733-2474.

MINNESOTA: *Twin Cities,* 416 Landmark Center, 75 W. 5th St., St. Paul 55102; Ken Green, 612-484-7478; **Hotline:** 612-633-0329.

MISSOURI: *Great River,* Hannibal; *Kansas City* **Hotline:** 816-333-2227. *St. Louis,* 3934 Flora Pl, 63110; **Hotline:** 314-771-7310.

NEBRASKA: *Omaha,* 1110 Howard St, 68102.

NORTH DAKOTA: *Great Plains,* 112 Avenue E, W. Bismarck 58501, 701-223-3492.

OHIO: *Central Ohio,* Box 20128, Columbus 43220. *Columbus,* 709 College Ave., 43209. *Hamilton* (Little Chicago), Arts Council, 319 W. 3rd, 45011, 513-863-8873. *Kent* (Early Jas), 7289 Route 43, 44240, 216-673-2297. *Peninsula,* 6105 Riverview Rd., 44264. *Southwestern Ohio,* Box 653, Cincinnati 45201.

WISCONSIN: *La Crosse,* Box 30811, 54602; Wayne Arihood, 608-788-5775. *Madison,* Box 8866, 53708; Linda Marty, 608-256-6310. *Milwaukee* (Unlimited), Box 92012, 53202. *River City,* Box 222, Eau Claire 54702; Jane Schley, 715-834-2864.

Center), 380 Lafayette St., 10003, 212-505-5660. **Hotline:** 718-465-7500. *New York Swing,* Box 2480, 10009. *Rockland County,* 33 Cragmere Rd., Suffern 10901. *Stony Brook* (International Art), 5 Saywood La., 11790, 516-632-6590. *Syracuse,* 201 Euclid Dr., Fayetteville 13066; Pat Carroll, 315-446-9189. *Duke Ellington Society,* Box 31, New York 10008. *Glenn Miller Society,* 301 E. 79th St. #17J, New York 10021. *Django Reinhardt Society,* Box 6610, New York 10150, 212-535-3933.

PENNSYLVANIA: *Allegheny,* 283 Jefferson St., Meadville 16335; Joe Boughton, 814-724-2163. *Central Pa.,* Box 889, Harrisburg 17108; Jack Snavely, 717-761-4000; **Hotline:** 717-533-2645. *Easton,* 2190 Gateway Terr. #203A, 18042; Bud Shaffer, 215-646-0980. *N. Warren,* 107 S. State St., 16365; Hal Putnam, 814-723-1795. *Philadelphia* (Penn-Jersey), 8511 Benton Ave., 19152; Joe Seigle, 215-745-6285. *Philadelphia Swing,* 215-248-2208. *Quakertown* (Fugowees), Box 457, 18951; Bob Grayson, 215-797-8822.

WEST VIRGINIA: *Charleston,* 1430 Quarrier St., 25301. *Coon-Sanders Nighthawks,* 202 10th St., Kenova 25530, 304-453-2254.

## *SOUTH*

FLORIDA: *Central Florida;* Karen Short, 407-295-7743. *Clearwater* (Al Downing's), 1616 S. Jefferson Ave., 33516. *Cocoa Beach,* 336 Carmine Dr., 32931; Alan Simms, 305-784-3616. *Fort Myers,* 11610 Caravel Circle S.W. #203, 33908. *Gainesville,* Box 12769, 32604; Stephen Langer, 904-335-1748. *Largo* (Suncoast Dixieland), Box 1014, 34649; David Hampton, 813-443-3012. *Palm Beach,* 213 N. Dixie Hwy., Lake Worth 33460, 407-533-1025. *Pensacola,* Box 18337, 32523; George Evans, 904-455-8622. *Plantation* (Hot Jazz & Alligator Gumbo), 1048 S.W. 49th Terrace, 33317; Will Connolly, 305-791-6183. *Sarasota,* c/o Theatre of the Arts, 61 N. Pineapple Ave., 34236, 813-366-1552. *Tampa Bay,* Box 290632, Tampa 33687. *Vero Beach* (Treasure Coast), Box 4003, 32964.

GEORGIA: *Coastal,* Box 8004, Savannah 31412.

LOUISIANA: *New Orleans,* 828 Royal St. #265, 70016; Donald Marquis, 504-525-9910.

MISSISSIPPI: *Coast,* 417 Walda Dr., Biloxi 39531; L.E. Swetman, 601-374-1081. *Jackson* (New Bourbon), Box 4545, 39216; Chuck Allen, 601-982-5712.

NORTH CAROLINA: *Charlotte,* Box 37002, 28237. *North Carolina Jazz Festival,* 1924 S. 16th St., Wilmington 28401; Harry van Velsor, 919-762-5207.

SOUTH CAROLINA: *Columbia,* Box 811, 29202; Bob Davis, 803-799-8695.

TENNESSEE: *Memphis,* 4607 Boyce Rd., 38117; Robert DeShields, 901-685-6193. *Nashville,* Box 121293, 37212; John Dorsey, Jr., 615-298-3912.

## LOCAL JAZZ—JAZZ SOCIETIES

The American Federation of Jazz Societies was formed in 1984 of affiliated jazz societies in the United States and Canada. Its purpose: "to perpetuate jazz and retain a grasp of the historic elements that make our music so important." The oldest society is the New Orleans Jazz Society, founded in 1948. The second oldest is the California Hot Jazz Society, founded by Floyd Levin in 1949. The societies hold meetings, dances, and concerts, and sometimes sponsor museums, halls of fame, instruction, and other activities. Some have specific interests, such as ragtime, dixieland, or swing. Below is a listing of jazz societies across North America as of May 1989, along with jazz hotlines.

### NORTHEAST

CONNECTICUT: *Connecticut* (Federation), Box 11598, Newington 06111, 203-666-7043. *Connecticut* (Traditional), Box 730, Woodbury 07698; Robert Najarian, 203-634-0135. *Coon-Sanders Nighthawks*, 349 Rye St., Broad Brook 06016; Bob Harrington, 203-582-0322.

MASSACHUSETTS: *Boston Swing*, Box 674, Watertown. *Cape Cod*, 62 Center St, Dennisport; Marie Marcus, 617-398-2945; **Hotline:** 617-432-5453. *Western Mass.* (Washington Hall), Box 287, Greenfield 01302; George Corsiglia, 413-772-0164.

NEW HAMPSHIRE: *N.H. Library*, 56 Londonderry Tpk., Auburn 03032, 603-622-6939.

### MIDATLANTIC

DISTRICT OF COLUMBIA: *Washington* (Potomac River), 3608 35th St. N.W., 20016; Don Farwell, 202-244-0843; **Hotline:** 703-698-PRJC. *Duke Ellington Society*, 913 Hamilton St. N.E., Washington, 20011; Terrell Allen, 202-529-5972.

MARYLAND: *Baltimore Swing*, 301-889-5731. *Washington Swing*, 3901 Upshur St, Brentwood 20722; Anita Schubert, 301-565-0104.

NEW JERSEY: *New Jersey*, 504 Vanderveer Rd., Bridgewater 08807; Warren Vaché, 201-388-8905. *Central Jersey*, 718 O'Hagan Terr., Neptune 07753; J.G. Johnson, 201-922-2035. *Delaware Valley*, 400 Windsor Dr., Bellmawr 08031; John Smith, 609-933-0571.

NEW YORK: *Buffalo* (Queen City), 849 Delaware Ave. #203, 14209; Thomas Lanphear, 716-634-1863. *Long Island*, Box 1242, W. Babylon 11704; Howie Weinmann, 516-669-6152. *New York* (Jazz

night
lights

1955

## READING ABOUT JAZZ

No writers nor the words they use can be a substitute for hearing the actual sounds of jazz itself. Mere words would be like describing the color red to a blind man. There is also the problem that so much of what is written and recalled about jazz is often myth and legend: the addled memory of the old wrapped in nostalgia.

The list of books which follows is a good, basic one, and the author of this book has found these volumes helpful in cross-checking dates and titles, and comparing conflicting data.

If you want it *all* under one title, there is the really BIG two volumes that cost three hundred dollars and consist of over a thousand pages: *The New Grove Dictionary of Jazz.* It tells you all you will ever want to know about jazz, and maybe more. If you can't afford to own it, you should be able to find it in larger public and university libraries.

| | |
|---|---|
| The Sound of Surprise | Whitney Balliett |
| The World of Duke Ellington | Stanley Dance |
| The Encyclopedia of Jazz | Leonard Feather |
| Celebrating the Duke and Louie | Ralph Gleason |
| Jazz Talk | Robert S. Gold |
| The Reluctant Art | Benny Green |
| Jazz Is | Nat Hentoff |
| Jazz: Its Evolution and Essence | André Hodeir |
| Storyville to Harlem | S. Longstreet |
| Beneath the Underdog | Charles Mingus |
| Bird! The Legend of Charlie Parker | Robert Reisner |
| Early Jazz | Gunther Schuller |
| The Jazz Tradition | Martin Williams |
| Chasing the Trane | Martin Williams |

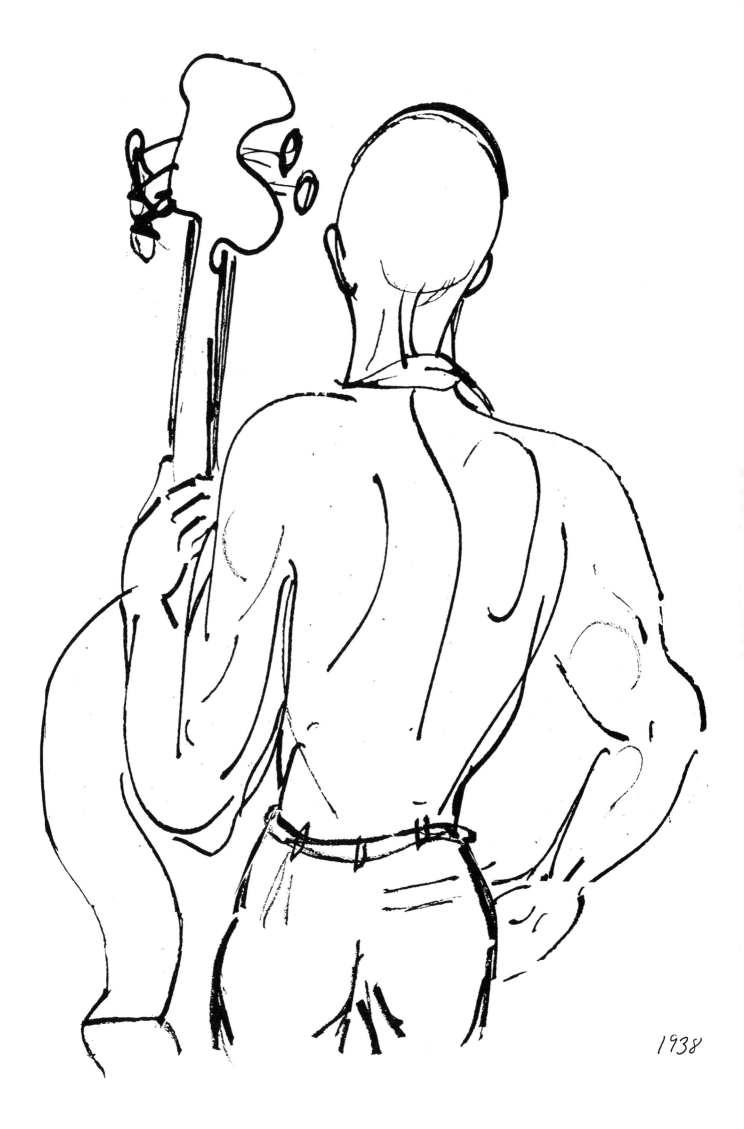

1938

| | |
|---|---|
| Diz and Getz | Blue Note |
| Bud Powell, Vol. 1 | Atlantic |
| The Avant Garde (Coltrane/Cherry) | Milestone |
| Thelonious Monk in Person | Capitol |
| Birth of the Cool (Miles Davis) | United Artists |
| Miles Davis | Impulse |
| Mingus Plays Piano | Polydor |
| Ornette Coleman Trio | Columbia |
| Shakti with John McLaughlin | Verve |

## THE ESSENTIAL RECORDINGS

| | |
|---|---|
| Scott Joplin | Biograph |
| Negro Songs - "Leadbelly" | Musiccraft |
| Dixieland Jazz | Decca |
| King Oliver's Jazz Band | Smithsonian |
| New Orleans Jazz | Decca |
| Johnny Dobbs and Kid Ory | Epic |
| Immortal Ma Rainey | Milestone |
| Original James P. Johnson | Folkways |
| Boogie-Woogie Piano Solos | Victor |
| Louis Armstrong Story | Columbia |
| Chicago Jazz | Decca |
| Bix Beiderbecke and the Wolverines | Hot Record Soc. |
| Bix Beiderbecke Legend | RCA |
| Sidney Bechet, Vol. 1 | Vogue |
| Blue Bechet | Columbia |
| Immortal Fletcher Henderson | Milestone |
| Ellington in Newport | Columbia |
| Duke Ellington - The Pianist | Fantasy |
| Art Tatum Masterpieces | MCA |
| Valentine Stomp (Fats Waller) | RCA |
| The Immortal Django Reinhardt | GNP |
| Dixie (Jimmy) Dorsey | RCA |
| Tribute to (Tommy) Dorsey | Columbia |
| Artistry in Rhythm (Stan Kenton) | Capitol |
| The Red Nichols Story | Brunswick |
| Best of Count Basie | Columbia |
| Benny Goodman in Moscow | RCA |
| Benny Carter | Prestige |
| The Billie Holiday Story | Decca |
| The Best of Ella | MCA |
| Sarah Vaughan | Everest |
| Fats Domino Swings | Columbia |
| Genius of Gerry Mulligan | Folkways |
| The Very Best of Bird | Warners |

## *LISTENING TO JAZZ*

It is a problem in collecting music from the history of jazz to decide not only what to collect, but also in what form. The reproduction of music is still in the process of revolutionary change. Should one collect LPs (long-playing records), CDs (compact discs), or cassette tapes, with or without images? And what will tomorrow bring? What new processes are in work to further confuse the collector? If you make your own tapes, how true can such recordings be in nuance and tonal depth to the originals? Recently, CDs have become the favorite of serious jazz fans and jazz recording companies, but they are expensive and often out of range for the more occasional fan.

Listed here is a good selection of the history of the jazz and its masters on LPs, but many of them are also available on CDs and cassettes. The changeover in sound reproduction is so rapid that you may not find some of the titles in the form you prefer even in the best record stores. For some, you may have to hunt in places that stock oldies and used albums. It may be best to work with the newest catalogs issued by recording companies, and try to come as close as possible to the titles of the masterworks of the great jazz players.

If you don't know where to start and you can afford it, you might buy *The Smithsonian Collection of Classic Jazz*. It holds 96 recordings from Jelly Roll Morton to the World Saxophone Quartet; it comes in LP ($50), cassette ($50), and CD ($60) forms; and it has a valuable text put together by Martin Williams. The address is Smithsonian Books and Recordings, P.O. Box 10229, Des Moines, IA 50381, or call 800-678-2677.

'51

Hangover Club, L.A.
1941

# Z

## BOB ZURKE (BOGUSLAW ZUKOWSKI)
(1911?-1944)

He came out of Detroit, a fine jazz pianist known for his BOOGIE-WOOGIE piano. In 1936, he was with Bob Crosby's *Bob Cats.* Zurke was also to work with Meade "Lux" Lewis and Pete Johnson; he was always dependable. In 1941, again with Bob Crosby, he was the featured soloist at the Hangover Club in Los Angeles.

# Z

## THE ZOOT SUIT

Like Topsy, it "just growed" from CAB CALLOWAY's way-out "set of threads": football-sized shoulder pads, pants with extra-baggy knees and tight around the shoe tops. Topped by a flat-topped hat with a brim as wide as a bike tire. To which outfit was added an extra-large key chain at least a yard long, and two-toned shoes. Harlem and other big cities soon had special zoot tailors who were specialists in the extra-wide lapels, the high-hitched pants. Most of the zoot suits were worn by jazz-loving males, street gangs, and almost as uniforms by members who hung out in juke box clubs or joints. By the 1950s, the zoot suit fashion had pretty much passed its popularity. Then in the 1980s, a modified zoot suit was seen on band platforms and TV comics. A very loose, tent-like jacket, wide trousers, baggy to an extreme. However, the wide-brimmed hat and the two-toned shoes were missing.

# Y

## LESTER WILLIS "PRES" YOUNG (1909-1959)

All the family were musical. He was a drummer as a kid in his father's band. Born in Mississippi, but growing up in New Orleans, he took to the tenor saxophone. In the early 1930s, he was working with KING OLIVER and FLETCHER HENDERSON, and went on to COUNT BASIE's Reno Club. He formed a personal attachment with BILLIE HOLIDAY, and recorded with her; it was she who called him "Pres." During the war years in the army he spent a year in the stockade for using drugs. His playing was good but not as it had been, and he was in lots of hospitals. In 1959, he played in Paris and died a day after he landed in the U.S.A.

## THE WOLVERINES

They were the first import white jazz group in Chicago that got attention. Teenagers out of Austin High School. Bud Freeman, Frank Teschemacher, Jim Lanigan, Dan Tough, Jim and Dick McPartland—BIX BEIDERBECKE drifted in and out. Using a heavy beat, dissonance and quarter notes. They started at the Stockton Club near Hamilton, Ohio, in 1923. A college kid named Hoagy Carmichael hired them for a college dance. He kept hiring them, and Bix was the star, when sober. In 1927, the Wolverines were recording "Nobody's Sweetheart," "Bullfrog Blues." They went on to become history, all but Teschemacher. He stepped in front of a car.

# W

## TEDDY WILSON (1912-1986)

He was born in Austin, Texas, and his mother and father were teachers at Tuskegee Institute. He listened at the school to collections of FATS WALLER, LOUIS ARMSTRONG, BIX BEIDERBECKE. He played piano early. He was impressed by groups like FLETCHER HENDERSON'S, *McKinney's Cotton Pickers*. He met ART TATUM, and took professionally to the piano. Teddy impressed BENNY CARTER and ended up on a road tour with Louis Armstrong. The jazz historian, John Hammond, got Teddy to record small combo sessions with BILLIE HOLIDAY. In 1936, Teddy was with BENNY GOODMAN'S *Trio*. He then had a band of his own. Later he appeared in the movie *The Benny Goodman Story*. He traveled a great deal, going from playing at CAFE SOCIETY to join the group at Monroe's Uptown Club.

1929

### PAUL WHITEMAN, "THE KING OF JAZZ"
(1890-1967)

It was easy to get fame and a title with the right press agent and a public misinformed of the true facts. Whiteman was a popular dance leader, with the jolly frame of a fat man. He had no true base in jazz, but did employ BIX, THE DORSEYS, Teagarden and other true jazz figures. But they had to play Whiteman arrangements. He commissioned GERSHWIN's "Rhapsody In Blue."

Longstreet
Fats Waller '33

# W

## THOMAS "FATS" WALLER (1904-1943)

He came from Kansas City, as so many early jazzmen did. Fats took to the piano, and to derby hats and writing music. In New York he worked with Bessie Smith, Sarah Martin, and also as a soloist. In 1929, he did the music for the black Harlem stage review *Connie's Hot Chocolates.* He toured Europe in 1937 and remained known as the author of his kind of songs: gay, lilting and half mocking. "A Fats Waller tune was like a signature." He wrote "Honeysuckle Rose," "Ain't Misbehavin'," "Stealin' Apples," and "Alligator Crawl." In the 1980s, long after Fats' death, a stage show called *Ain't Misbehavin'* featured "Fats Waller" and company to great popular success.

# V

## THE VILLAGE VANGUARD

The *New Yorker* called it "the greatest jazz club in the world." It is a tiny cellar at 178 Seventh Avenue, opened in 1935. Its owner was Max Gordon (1903-1989), the patron saint of jazz in the Big Apple. Max favored classical jazz and kept rock-fusion-jazz at bay. The club has always been open every night and most of the jazz greats have either played there or been regular patrons. Too small to make it a money success, it was said, "this place has never made a dime." In New York City, a club that uses music is called a "room;" to old customers and performers, Max's place is known as "the cellar." Max also ran a swank club, the Blue Agent, where the singers were called *chanteuses*, but it never was as warm to jazz lovers as the Vanguard.

Sarah
Vaughan,
recording
"Young Man"
with D "334
and Bird -
1945

SL
1945

# V

**SARAH VAUGHAN** (1924-    )

She was discovered as a young Baptist church singer in Newark, New Jersey. She had studied for a decade to become a pianist. In 1942, she won an amateur singing contest in Harlem, which led to her becoming a vocalist for EARL HINES' band. She was unique in her harmony and rhythm and attracted to the sounds of GILLESPIE and PARKER. She began to record for Columbia, Mercury, at times using pop commercial music (Mancini, Legrand). Her jazz vocals remain amazing in range and sensitivity.

*V*

## USO

**A**n organization of show people, musicians, and enter-tainers who toured the war fronts of World War II, across the Atlantic and the Pacific, performing for the soldiers and sailors under primitive conditions. Jazz groups were among the most popular. A War Department recording organization, "Armed Forces Radio," broadcast music and shows to scattered remote areas. Jazz and senti-mental blues were among the most in demand by the forces.

# T

## *LENNIE TRISTANO* (1919-1978)

At seven, although born blind, he taught himself the piano. At twelve, he was playing pro, and later worked with club bands and dance groups. One of the best-educated musicians of the era, he taught music and could improvise Bach. In 1949, with a small personal group, he recorded improvised atonal music: "Digression" and "Intuition." He played pure piano, no dubbing or tape overlaps. By the 1970s, modern jazz owed him a great deal. Some have called his atonal sound "Free Jazz." Like some virtuosos, his following was small and choice.

# T

## THE TRIMMINGS

**F**ashion was very important to the jazz player, singer or composer, as well as the loyal fan. For a time, large shades with very dark lenses matched a huge Afro hairdress (now pretty much subdued). The bold musician favored a beret, or the extra small felt hat with the very narrow brim. For each individual, the greatest creation was the hair and mustache. A combination mustache and modified Vandyke was popular, trending often to Fu Manchu or Mexican bandit. A pocket chain, nearly a yard long to twirl on a finger, was the Phi Beta Kappa key of jazz and, if affordable, gold for wrists, neck, and an earring was the finishing touch. What importance did this have for serious jazz? DUKE ELLINGTON: "It's not just body trimming, it's the symbol, it's something different and worth advertising; it's the warning that once you pay attention, all fashion becomes in time history." (see ZOOT SUIT)

Nite Club

1940

# T

## TIN PAN ALLEY

The Alley is a mythical place in New York City where popular tunesmiths were supposed to have written the early hit songs. People, most of them, are touched by the recall of "our song," which animates the emotions on simple but strong levels: love songs, ballads, laments, romantic nostalgia. Irving Berlin, Jerome Kern, Arthur Schwartz, Jule Styne were the masters of this form of music. Some, like GERSHWIN with "Swanee River," composed imitation black songs for Al Jolson. Jolson, a great entertainer working in black face, sustained these false jazz songs long past the time when the true jazz was already here. However, much of this material can be turned to the use of jazz bands by rearranging and improvising the melodic forms. So they are often annexed as jazz classics. Many bands often mix pop and true jazz, and singers have become famous by singing both pop and jazz. LOUIS ARMSTRONG and BILLIE HOLIDAY could turn a pop tune to their own patterns.

# T

### ART TATUM (1910-1956)

What do you say when you are called "the greatest jazz pianist that ever lived"? Art Tatum was born blind in one eye and with little sight left in the other. A music school for the blind saw his talent, and as a teenager he had his own band. At 22, the singer Adelaide Hall took him to New York, where he made a living as a soloist. He toured the country and then Europe, usually as a soloist. By 1943, he had a trio. Tatum went his own way musically, he played lines his way, chords were for him items to play with and juggle about. He could take pop and make it sound impressive; rearrange them, whip them with original ideas. No one seemed to be able to improvise his way. He died still making chords dance brilliantly.

# T

## TAP DANCING

The great dancer, Bill "Bojangles" Robinson, always insisted that tap dancing began when barefooted Southern plantation hands came to town with their first pair of shoes, "which they tested on their feet by tapping them on the wooden floor." Perhaps it's true. But fact or not, the sound of leather on wood, with added steel toe-taps, set to music, became an art. Buck, of the tap dancing wonders Buck and Bubbles, insisted, "Tap dancin' and jazz, why they belong together like ham and eggs." From sidewalk buck-and-wing to the polished tappers of such early Harlem shows as *Hot Chocolates,* to the kingpin showplace of vaudeville, the Palace on Broadway, tap dancers put jazz to the test as the inspiration of their metal-clad toes and clicking heels. The tradition of tap continues with specialists Gregory Hines, Harold Nicholas, Jimmy Slyde, Sandman Sims, Bunny Briggs, Steve Condos, Arthur Duncan and Pat Rice.

*S*

## SWING

**B**asic to swing is the antic use of rhythm, a recharting of the continuity of the music, putting in a tempo with a pulse of its own. It's not something that can be fully arranged on paper; it's the way you play it. It was the most popular form of jazz with the public. It touched bases with ragtime, the blues, got going in the the late 1920s, when the saxophone set the tone with the slapped bass, and was in great demand into the mid-1940s. JELLY ROLL MORTON's "Kansas City Stomp" was an early form, and his *Red Hot Peppers,* as was ELLINGTON's "It Don't Mean a Thing If It Ain't Got That Swing." GOODMAN, Hawkins, JIMMY AND TOMMY DORSEY did popular arrangements. Artie Shaw held a "Swing Music Concert." The young who became addicted to the music began to be called "swingers," and "swinging" entered the language. Swing favored BIG BANDS, and it was splendid music to dance to, but it declined as it turned sweetly romantic. It had moved too far from the toughness of solid jazz.

Longstreet.
1987

*S*

## STRIDE

It was a form of jazz that took over a lot of the pace and rhythm of RAGTIME, with gay music and a heavy base. The pioneer of stride piano was JAMES P. JOHNSON, who led Eubie Blake and Willie "The Lion" Smith into the fold. His greatest follower, younger and bolder, was FATS WALLER, who produced such classics as "Ain't Misbehavin'" and "Honeysuckle Rose." He also brought a certain soft tender touch to the stride piano—and even to the organ. Stride music got some of its piano ideas and techniques across the ocean from Europe. It refreshed jazz and had to, if the music was not to become stagnant.

1982
Longstreet

*S*

## STORYVILLE

The sporting house district in NEW ORLEANS was set aside in 1897, by an ordinance presented by Alderman Sidney Story, as an uninhabited living section of the city open to brothels. This section of the French Quarter was confined by the Custom House and St. Louise Street and North Basin and Robertson. The "madames" named it Storyville in honor of the alderman ... "forty lively and jumpy blocks of vice and music, likker and laughter." As a now legal district, music could be introduced: the parlor piano, the banjo and guitar, aided by a cornet and trumpet for festive occasions like New Year's and the Fourth of July. At other times a banjo and piano served. The tunes were popular old favorites, but as most of the players hired were usually into early jazz, in time, "the sporting house music was often blowing real jazz," said JELLY ROLL MORTON, who had played in the houses. It was in 1917, when America went to war, that the War Department closed the sporting houses to keep the soldiers and sailors living clean. "It was all right to die for your country, but not to get laid for it," quipped Nell Kimball, a New Orleans madame. Many of the jazzmen, now out of work, began to drift north to CHICAGO and HARLEM.

_S_

## STAGE SHOWS

Harlem produced the first all-black stage shows that became famous. _Hot Chocolates_ had the voice of Ethel Waters and the music of FATS WALLER, as did the _All Negro Review, Blackbird of 1928,_ and _Chocolate Dandies_. Fats again did the music for _Harlem Fuss_ and later _Black Bird Bye Bye, I'll Arrive Late Tonight._ These shows featured singing, dancing, comedy, and produced JOSEPHINE BAKER, Lena Horne, Bill Robinson and many others. Many of these shows ended up on Broadway, others stayed in Harlem. There were always plans for black jazz shows. Most are now forgotten, but all were loud and active and full of hope. As one player said, "Hope is maybe the only sin."

_S_

## SPASM BANDS

In New Orleans groups sprang up soon after jazz became a form of entertainment: kids who played for coins
in the streets, on sidewalks outside clubs, cafés and
dance halls; small groups often aged from eight to
fifteen, and some older who played for the change
tossed to them. Ragged, tough, some of them were
actually very good, but many were just noisemakers. A
group could be made up of a battered cornet, a guitar,
sometimes a bass or a trombone, often a washboard,
wine jug, or suitcase. One or two might add a voice.
Some even gained a sort of fame, like the _Razy Dazy
Spasm Band,_ who fought any group that tried to use
their name. They were on the scene on Fat Tuesday—
the Mardi Gras—or stationed in front of the Masonic Hall
or the Eagle Saloon, until the cops moved them on.

Paris - night club

# S

## *MARTIAL SOLAL* (1927-   )

**J**azz spread quickly around the world. Solal was born in Algiers and as a small boy was already at the piano. In 1950, he was in Paris in the middle of the frantic jazz scene and actively playing with the best, even with Americans such as SIDNEY BECHET, STAN GETZ and Kenny Clarke. He began to write music, did at least forty scores for movies and was a popular piano soloist. Some thought him "the best jazz man at the piano in Europe." He moved in many directions. Wrote suites like "Rhythmical Escape" and "Ah Non," an ironic tour de force. He could combine swing with a sense of humor. His tone was usually trim and neat, but he could also produce complicated work that shattered musical patterns. Work where tempos clash against each other.

1950

## SHOWBOAT JAZZ

While the early showboats on the Mississippi used the music of ragtime, popular tunes, and minstrels before their era passed, many turned to jazz as the trek north of the jazz men increased. Some of it was not pure jazz, but as surviving players recalled it, a lot of it was. The river towns, where the showboats played, were prime centers of the music and it was welcomed by the patrons, who had grown up with the music and often played it themselves.

*S*

## SCAT SINGING

The credit goes to LOUIS ARMSTRONG as the inventor of scat singing, which is nothing more than making meaningless sounds to music: "Bop-a-de-hop-scop" or "bing-bing-bang-bing-deedle-do-bing-bop." Louis claims he forgot the lyrics one night while performing and went into a jabberwocky of sound. It caught on and other soloists went for it. Slim Gaillard in "Flat Foot Floogie" and "Cement Mixer." It certainly has humor and a mocking tone that keeps jazz from getting too serious. DIZZY GILLESPIE was as good as Louie as a scat singer. In Paris, the *Double Six* did it as "Bop-scop-à-la-bop." There was a version called "vocalese." Scat sounded like Gertrude Stein in Eddie Jerrson's "I'm in the Mood for Love."

Chain gang
Camp

Georgia

'33

# R

## ROOTS

Blacks were in the United States *before* the *Mayflower* or the Virginia planters. They had early roots in the French and Spanish colonies and were the forefathers of what was to become jazz. They were on the soil from New England to Florida for two to three hundred years. As slaves they were not taught to read or write. But the Christians gave them their God, and hymns to glorify Him. Blacks turned these into spirituals. Then in despair and loneliness, they turned the agony of their lives into laments that were tinged blue: field songs, work songs, jail songs. Their instruments were flutes, fiddles, and drums, in various shapes and kinds. Their music went from "Let My People Go" to "Swing Low, Sweet Chariot" to "Lost Woman Blues," "John Henry," "Jailhouse Walls." Slowly, between the end of the Civil War and the new century, all this began to gel into the first sounds of jazz, an evolution from all that had gone before into an original way of expressing existence.

1974

# R

## THEODORE WALTER "SONNY" ROLLINS
(1929-    )

Only when in a New York City high school did Rollins feel the pull, becoming a serious saxophone player. He first played alto, then tenor sax—and rubbing against BOP, he gained a strong dedicated sound. He played with BUD POWELL, MILES DAVIS and CHARLIE PARKER. In 1957, Rollins had his own group, but he vanished for three years ... where was Sonny Rollins? Then someone saw him playing on the Williamsburg Bridge. In 1962, he was back in public view with an LP, *The Bridge.* He has vanished and returned several times. Wrote the hit "Alfie," also "The Cutting Edge." He always seems just a bit ahead of what is coming.

# R

## JEAN BAPTISTE "DJANGO" REINHARDT
(1910-1953)

He was a real Gypsy with a wandering tribe; born in a Belgian village. Self-taught on the banjo and the guitar, a master in his teens even though he lost the use of two fingers in a fire. By 1933, somehow he had found jazz and was playing with groups in Paris. Two years later, the Hot Club of France was formed and Django began playing with violinist Stéphane Grapelly. He was also recording such items as "Dinah" and "Tiger Rag." By 1946, he was touring the United States with DUKE ELLINGTON. Between heavy drinking and high blood pressure, his health was in decline. At his best, playing European and American jazz, his way was sure, clean and very original with a grace very much his own. He did some composing of a sad beauty, "Nuages," as well as "Micro" (Mike) and "Black Night." His style of jazz was very influential; most later players of the guitar owe much to him. While fishing one day, Django died of a stroke.

# R

## ANDY RAZAF (ANDREAMENENTANIA RAZAFKERIEFO) (1895-1973)

Few people even among earnest jazz fans can recall the name Andy Razaf. He was said to be the son of a Malagasy nobleman. Razaf wrote the lyrics of over 500 popular songs, such as "Ain't Misbehavin'," "Honeysuckle Rose," "S'posin'," "The Joint Is Jumping," "Stompin' at the Savoy," and a hundred other standards. He worked with FATS WALLER, Eubie Blake, W.C. Handy. He started as a writer of salacious and amusing texts: "If I Can't Sell It, I'll Keep Sitting on It." He went on to do "Black and Blue" for the show *Hot Chocolates*. You still have to hunt for his name on much popular music.

c. 1928

### GERTRUDE MALISSA NIX PRIDGETT "MA" RAINEY (1886-1939)

Maybe those weren't all real names. It sounds like her. She married "Pa," William Rainey, who produced minstrel shows, black vaudeville and all kinds of shows for southern and northern Negroes. It was Ma who found a hungry kid named Bessie Smith and put her in Pa's *Rabbit Foot Minstrels.* Ma had made the musical rounds and knew the power of her voice. She was a show woman in her own right and organized *Ma Rainey's Georgia Band* and *Ma Rainey's Tub Jub and Washboard Band.* She was called "The Mother of the Blues Generation," a force to bring black sound forward, to make the Negro aware he had something unique that he himself had created. Her best vocals are on recordings from 1923 to 1928: "Barrel House Blues," "See See Rider Blues," "Moonshine Blues," "Deep Moanin' Blues." In the late 1980s, there was a musical play about Ma, and a television drama. Good tries but not the real Ma. (see RACE RECORDS)

from 1900 film

# R

## *RAGTIME*

The forerunner of jazz began as a piano style in the late 1880s, and it was still popular in 1918 when jazz was replacing it as the new sound. One could party or dance to it, and ragtime lent itself to concerts, on stage and riverboats. It is highly syncopated music with a shifting sense of rhythm and pleasant, controlled melodic lines. It is best known through composer and pianist SCOTT JOPLIN. It shifts its accents, and its melodies are delightful. TIN PAN ALLEY took much of its style from ragtime, but of course never had its purity. Ragtime changed, spread itself, took on blue notes and tones of swing. Scott Joplin's "Maple Leaf Rag" is its most recalled tune. JELLY ROLL MORTON brought it into jazz. Jazz never did do away with ragtime completely. It was in popular demand for a long time.

# R

## RACE RECORDS

**W**hen at the turn of the century Mr. Edison's phonograph became popular, everything from grand opera to comic dialogue was recorded. "Race records" were made for the Negro trade and did not appear in white record shops. They recorded early MA RAINEY, Bessie Smith, and popular jazz groups from black theaters. The rest of the population was hardly aware of them. Later, collectors tried to hunt for them, but a great deal has been lost. Race records are not to be confused with "Coon" music such as "Coontown Strutters Ball," which was the product of TIN PAN ALLEY popular songs. The term "coon" in those days was not considered a racial insult, even if it should have been. Fake "black" themes were in demand from "Mammy" to "Swanee".

1964

# P

## EARL "BUD" POWELL (1924-1966)

Like so many in jazz, he was born into a family of musicians, in New York City. At ten, he could play anything he had heard by his favorites, and as a teenager was playing piano at Coney Island. Meeting CHARLIE PARKER, he saw the light. In 1943, he was with the Cootie Williams group and part of the 52ND STREET jazz scene. He recorded solos and group playing for Verve and Blue Note. He was a victim of dope and booze, and his mind and body were affected. By twenty-one he had been in hospitals and sanitoriums; places he came to know well. He moved to Paris in 1959, and was active in French and American jazz there. Drink led to tuberculosis and malnutrition. In 1964, he was back in America, at Birdland, and then for the last two years of his life he played no more ... He did much to build BOP to fame.

on
grass

Cunningham 1988

P

## POT

It's been known as reefer, mufa, gauge, grass, dope. There was no law against its use when Latin-American music makers brought it into the country. And for some time there was open sale of pot in Harlem, on the streets. The jazz men and women found it a cheap way to face the hardships of their trade and life. Musicians claimed it aided their sense of music, the pacing, the release of their reactions to their playing. Is it harmful? Overuse of any item will do damage, but the jazz folk who have smoked pot—and almost all those contacted have, or do—claim that, if not used excessively, it does no harm. On the other hand, many medical people seem to think it is mind- and body-destroying.

P

### CHARLIE "BIRD" PARKER (1920-1955)

He came from Kansas City and was to astonish the jazz world and to suffer a tragic destiny. At eleven, he was playing saxophone, and he worked hard to become a master. He was with Buster Smith in 1937, and moved about perfecting an amazingly personal musical tone as a soloist. He was also on drugs. Drifting, he came to New York and ran into DIZZY GILLESPIE and Kenny Clarke, two other rebels—the three are given credit for creating BOP, and by 1945 were recording their music and its unique musical revolution. Still seeking the final form of bop. A year later he was in Camarillo State Hospital, a wreck. But released, he made some of his major recordings, toured abroad, played with Jazz at the Philharmonic. Drink and drugs were never discarded. He acted up in an odd manner and his music suffered at times. Charlie was in Bellevue. Let out, he made and broke dates. Was dead at 34. A genius, his influence rebuilt modern jazz.

*O*

## ORIGINS

Jazz was a new kind of music created by black
Americans mostly, at first, in the south, around New
Orleans, with a new kind of syncopated rhythm and
improvisations, with no rigid discipline or accepted texts.
Vocal styles on the instruments and flattened notes
made it different. As much invented as played, with off-
beat tone values and glissandos in fast sliding actions.
Also the repeating of phrases, called a riff. Short inter-
ludes, with improvised sections called breaks. It must be
heard for its tone and color phrasing, as so much
depends on what isn't set down, on the invention as it
is being played. Any text about it will only serve as an
introduction. The great jazz artists, men and women,
seem to create toward a new dimension of sound and
emotion that is beyond definition on a printed page. It
has its roots in pleasure, sorrow, sin, and awe of God,
in man's weakness and his hopes—material and
spiritual: the sad blue notes that suggest fulfillment can
be reached for but never captured.

old hot lips

1928

*O*

## JOSEPH "KING" OLIVER (1885-1938)

He came off a Louisiana plantation. He learned the cornet in New Orleans and played in the early bands: the *Olympia,* the *Eagle* and the *Magnolia.* Kid Ory named him "King." Moving to Chicago he added LOUIS ARMSTRONG to his band. He formed the *Creole Jazz Band* and the *Dixie Syncopators* and recorded his own compositions, like "Sugar Foot Stomp." He was an innovator of jazz improvisation, a free-swinging jazz style ... Times grew hard during the Depression, and he picked up gigs where he could. He was in poor health and he ended his life running a fruit stand. A true pioneer. There is still no stone on his grave in the Bronx.

1936

# N

### ERNEST LORING "RED" NICHOLS (1905-1965)

**B**orn in Utah, he was one of the best of the white jazz players and bandleaders. In 1925, he played the trumpet with such pop bands as those led by Vincent Lopez and PAUL WHITEMAN. He turned to the true jazz with the *Louisiana Rhythm Kings* and *Six Hottentots*. Finally, he formed his own group, *Red Nichols and His Five Pennies*. His was one of the first jazz bands to appear on radio, and he also lead theater orchestras on Broadway for *Strike Up the Band* and *Girl Crazy*. Nichols is an example of the true jazz bandleader who, to survive, had to divide his time between popular theater and radio work and the jazz that still survives on his many recordings.

# N

## NEWPORT JAZZ FESTIVAL

The Newport annual gathering is the best known of the jazz festivals. In 1956, DUKE ELLINGTON was the star attraction. LOUIS ARMSTRONG also came and said "I'm the audience myself ... don't like to hear myself play bad." Newport has had its good years and its so-so years. Also some infighting among its sponsors and temperamental stars. It got so bad that in 1973 it became "Newport in New York" as the festival searched for new playing fields, but it is back on the tracks, back again at Newport blasting the classical sounds and newer rock-jazz-fusion up at the stars. As jazz took many forms from swing to bop, to cool jazz, to funk and back, Newport has always been full of clashing opinions.

# N

## NEW ORLEANS JAZZ HERITAGE FESTIVAL

For over twenty years now, this festival has attracted great jazz with just an added touch of tourist hype. The word Festival can attract the real and true *and* the phony and the sleazy promoters. New Orleans has star talent and the years have seen some of the best jazz around. This was the town from which most of the first jazz notes came. Here was its start as the real thing. And here, too, the glitz of the New Orleans of big bucks has created myths. But there is a large bronze statue of LOUIS ARMSTRONG out in the street ... and the festival has continued to produce top jazz events, stars and groups all through May. MILES DAVIS, Max Roach, George Benson and Wynton Marsalis; blues performers Robert Cray, Etta James, Bobby "Blue" Bland, and the Fabulous Thunderbirds; purveyors of the New Orleans sound. The Neville Brothers, Fats Domino, the Radiators and Dr. John.

# N

## NEW ORLEANS

It began as a 'gator swamp—up from the delta of the Mississippi, Indians were there before the French came in 1762, but the Spanish took the town and Napoleon, who didn't own it, sold it to the U.S.A. It was a cotton port, a sporting house town, a riverboat station between itself and St. Louis. The bordellos needed music for their trade and that went from the colonial reel to Stephen Foster, to ragtime and at last to jazz. On festive evenings and holidays, a sporting house usually had a group consisting of a trumpet, a piano player, a banjo and a clarinet or guitar. Many later famous jazz players claimed to have begun in the sporting houses. When the War Department closed the places in 1917, the move was to CHICAGO. (see STORYVILLE)

1985

# N

## NAMES FOR JAZZ

First it was spelled jass, then it became jazz. But along the way it was talked of as jazzbo, jabo, jazzation, jazzanola, jazarella, jazzanjaz. One critic labeled its study "jazzology." All these are now out of date. Today the talk is of terms like COOL JAZZ, FUSION jazz, avant garde jazz, free jazz, "the new thing." New names come and go with a shift in styles. Progressive jazz, Afro jazz, Afro-Eurasian Jazz have been attached to some experiments, if they fitted or not.

1988

# M

## GERRY MULLIGAN (1927-    )

You mix Irish with German and you get a gunpowder mixture. Even as an untaught boy, Gerry roamed about music, played saxophone, piano, flugelhorn, clarinet. He also tried composing and arranging. By 1944, he was arranging for Tommy Tucker, played sax with GENE KRUPA and others, and in 1949 recorded with MILES DAVIS the *Birth of COOL JAZZ* series. He lived in a basement and arranged music. Some found his arranging hard to take. A touchy, chip-on-the-shoulder style with a tough tempo and much improvising. By 1952, there was West Coast Jazz and Gerry was talking of "contrapuntal swing." There was always hard wit and humor in his music. He didn't care for sad jazz. Often he felt "a band shouldn't play just to record." Gerry remained an opinionated soloist. He did try having a big band of his own and found that led to lots of details that didn't have much to do with the music.

Longstreet

# M

**BENNIE MOTEN** (1894-1935)

**W**ho made Kansas City Style? Most agree it was Moten. It was rich jazz, hard-hitting with a two-note beat. Aged twelve, he was with a kids' band. He went from trumpet to the piano and to arranging. He was at his best creating bands that showed off his Kansas City blues. Moten was always busy—never without a gig or a piano arrangement or even several bands at the same time. He died at the age of 41, as if he'd been aware he had to do a lot in a short time.

# M

**FERDINAND JOSEPH "JELLY ROLL" MORTON**
(1885-1941)

Some have called him the greatest liar in jazz. He claimed to have created much of the early jazz, invented BOOGIE-WOOGIE piano, and been the source of many of the first songs. Yet some of his claims stand up. He was playing fine RAGTIME around the end of the nineteenth century before he turned to jazz and was among its first players. Jelly Roll composed "Memories of You" and "I'm Just Wild about Harry." He worked both ragtime and STRIDE piano into his compositions. He inspired such men as Eubie Blake, who, in the 1980s, reached nearly the age of 100, the last of those players who went back to the days of Jelly Roll Morton and his jumping bass and wandering melody.

# M

## MONTEREY JAZZ FESTIVAL

The most delightful setting of an annual jazz festival is the West Coast one on Monterey Bay, among the tall pines. It combines, said Ralph Gleason, the late great jazz critic, "the grace at times of a royal court, crossed with a gypsy encampment." In 1964, Charlie Mingus led off, and three years later there was the explosion of a new singer, Janis Joplin. She was surprising, and you knew she couldn't last at her pace. DIZZY GILLESPIE with his upturned trumpet was there, setting his Afro jazz notes ... At late hours the sound of some last notes on a muted horn and the smell of pot and a sea breeze makes this festival special.

1963

# M

### *THELONIOUS MONK* (1920-1982)

He grew up with the piano in New York City, and seems to have taught himself the 88 keys. He started playing with an evangelist; joining PARKER and GILLESPIE he was among the founders of BOP. But he kept to his idiosyncratic musical ways. He recorded with Blue Note, Riverside and Columbia, mostly his own compositions. "'Round Midnight," "Ruby, My Dear," and his theme, "Epistrophy." He created big bands for 1959 and 1963 concerts in New York, but it is his solo piano records that are truly special. His music is often understated, his harmony a personal, half-told secret. There has been no one like him in the history of jazz. When one has said the man is unique, one has placed him in his field.

# M

## MINSTREL SHOWS

These were in the main a white invention, caricatures of
an invented black life, full of "Rasus" humor, low wit,
cakewalks. Whites in blackface created the shashay
walk and the watermelon-and-fried-chicken dialogue as
attempts at humor. The music was mostly RAGTIME and
pop tunes, but there was a jazz theme to a lot of it, badly
understood. So popular were minstrel shows that when
black colleges sent a minstrel show to Europe, the black
men were not felt to be black or kinky-haired enough, so
they had to use burnt cork on their faces and wear
woolly wigs. Minstrel humor lasted well into the days of
radio, with such stars as Mossass and January, and its
invented dialect was still around in *Amos 'n' Andy.*

# M

## MICKEY MOUSE BAND

**A** mickey mouse is a band that's usually bad, often of high school or college boys. "Boogily-borgily" (not boogie-woogie) is to confuse the music. Some terms that confuse people new to jazz: to "brown off" is to break tempo; "dooley-squat" is a mess; "jim jam" is to react quickly; a "flare up" builds a chord; a "lick" is a "break" or hot jazz phrase. A "slump" is a glissando; "scooping pitch" or "bending" is to alter pitch between notes; "rebop" and "ripbop" is another way of saying, here's a different bop. (see JAZZ LANGUAGE)

1978

# M

## *JOHN McLAUGHLIN* or *MAHAVISHNU*
(1942-    )

He came out of Yorkshire, picked up his own way of playing the guitar and went on to play with rock and jazz groups in Britain. By 1969, he was in the U.S.A. with MILES DAVIS recording such albums as *In a Silent Way*. In 1971, he was head of his own group and under the spell of an Indian guru, Sri Chinmoy Kumar Chose, and he added an Indian drummer to the group. John became Mahavishnu, but remained a very fine guitar player who brought some of the sounds of Asia into jazz and the blues. Hindu dogma has so far not over-colored jazz, nor has jazz had much impact on the gods and the pious people of India. McLaughlin has been very active in the use of electronics and in affecting the sound of the music on stage and in recordings.

# L

## THE LOUIS ARMSTRONG HOUSE

In New York City, plan a trip to the Louis Armstrong House on 10th Street in Queens. It's now an official landmark—and there is a bronze plaque attached to the one-story house. It is a place full of "Pops" memorabilia, tapes, recordings, photographs and scrapbooks. To many jazz fans it's as vital to our history as the White House. It was Louie's long-time home base, but actually he was away on tours all over the world most of the year.

'72

# L

## LATIN-AMERICAN JAZZ

"Music, like love, is an exchange of something close and precious," DUKE ELLINGTON once said. "If it works, bull's-eye; if not, send it to the hock shop." So, as in a love relationship, jazz has influenced Latin-American music, and seen true jazz created in Brazil and Argentina. Also, out of Latin America have come the samba and the congo, the tango and the habañero, salsa and calypso, with beats and style that have added to the jazz sound. Argentina took to jazz early and today is represented by the work of Lalo Schifrin, both at the piano and composing the music for films. Brazil has its own style of jazz, using African and Indian influences; going heavy on the percussion. Jazz has greatly influenced Bossa Nova, a Brazilian form of jazz greatly enjoyed for dancing and a favorite style for such American jazzmen as STAN GETZ. Familiar to Americans are guitarist Laurindo Almeida, drummer Airto Moreira, and saxophonist Moacir Santos.

# K

**GENE KRUPA** (1909-1973)

To some he was the greatest of all jazz drummers, to others a master showman in his frenzy working the drums and traps. Born in the Windy City, by 1927 he was with the *McKenzie-Condon Chicagoans*, next year the *Chicago Rhythm Kings*; on the West Coast he drummed for RED NICHOLS at the Hollywood Restaurant. He later worked the drums with BENNY GOODMAN's *Charleston Chasers*. His own band was *Gene Krupa's Chicagoans*. Over the years he appeared with most of the great bands and the famous jazz leaders. The Krupa style on the skins was characterized by his flying hair and his violent attack with his drumsticks. No matter what some may have thought of his style, he was clearly a master drummer. A master of SWING sound, he was often featured by Goodman.

# K

## STAN KENTON (1912-1979)

One of the most modern of the white jazz figures in his day, Stan Kenton was born in Kansas. It is amazing how many of the white jazz players that became important were born far from the jazz-filled big cities. Most came to their devotion to the music through radio listening or stray recordings. Kenton did have a youth in Los Angeles and early, at age 16, was seeking work as an arranger. By 1941, he was known as a good pianist and arranger in the SWING era, being recorded by Decca and Capitol. With his own band, Kenton did "Artistry in Rhythm." He worked with vocalists Anita O'Day, June Christy, and Gene Howard. He was one of the innovators and experimenters of modern jazz and its ideas. In 1956, he went to England and elsewhere in the world. Age only slightly slowed him down.

## THE JUKE BOX

The box of chrome, stained glass, glitters, and its rack of recordings, is a hundred years old now, a collector's item. A Seeburg Model-C (1950) with Select-O-Matic gut, or a Wurlitzer 850 with glass tubes of bubbling colored liquid, can set you back from $500 to $4,000—if in working order. In 1986, an old Wurlitzer went for $6,500. The first juke box ate nickels, now they ask mostly for quarters. At their prime, when Caddies had fins, their iridescent plastic panels sheltered vacuum tubes, and there were no solid-state circuits—just BILLIE HOLIDAY singing "I'll See You in My Dreams."

Photo: 1911

### SCOTT JOPLIN (1868-1917)

He came from Texas, touched base in Missouri and then ended up in New York. Joplin was the greatest of the RAGTIME composers. He started publishing his music in 1895, and spent the rest of his life moving ragtime into various musical forms, from little songs to operas like *Tremonisha*. He is best remembered for "Maple Leaf Rag." Scott felt neglected while alive but came to fame long after he was buried. His music was used to score the film *The Sting*. He never could get his operas properly before the public, but in the 1980s, *Tremonisha* had a critical success.

Longstreet
c. 1942

## JAMES P. JOHNSON (1891-1955)

**B**orn in New Brunswick, New Jersey, Johnson's mother was a talented pianist. From her he got to play RAGTIME dance tunes, popular music. He played for the summer trade in Coney Island and Atlantic City. Hearing more of this new jazz, he was Bessie Smith's piano player, became a genuine STRIDE player, which led to his composing. He tried composing everything, even CHARLESTON, but also serious jazz, ballet music, tone poems and symphonies. He certainly moved ragtime towards jazz and boldly nailed it down. His best performing work was done as an accompanist. He was a serious original musician, a musician who came slowly to jazz from a fine piano background and, when he got to jazz, knew all contents and how to use them.

BUNK'S

JAZZ

from the 1940 Stephen Longstreet 3 color poster          1940

## WILLIAM GEARY "BUNK" JOHNSON
(1879-1949)

He proved you *can* go home again. An early jazzman, with the best. He was playing the cornet at eleven in New Orleans and soon was working as a professional. Some claim he was with BUDDY BOLDEN's group *The Eagle Band.* He went touring in 1903, drifting to the West Coast, playing about, a drifter. His brass tones became famous. Times turned hard. He lost his teeth and trumpet. He was rediscovered, promoted, and his sound was found as good as ever, as his recordings of "Bogalusa Strut" and "Panama" showed. He had a decade of true fame and became the hero who returned from obscurity to his rightful place in the jazz story.

## JAZZ LANGUAGE

Like Zen ("if you think you know Zen, it isn't Zen anymore") so jazz talk: as soon as it becomes public, the jazz folk drop it. Some terms stay: an "Uncle Tom" is a black who caters to whites; "woodshedding" is practicing; "dicty" is high-toned; "hincty" is snobbish, conceited. "Sea food, mama!" is a sexual proposition; a "shakeup" is mixed dregs of drinks; a "blip" is five cents; to "fake" is to improvise; a "ride-out" is to swing a chorus, or the final chorus itself; "box of teeth" an accordion; "wood pile" a xylophone; "cleek" a sad type; money is "bread", "moola" "lettuce," "long green," "gelt;" "boogie-woogie" used to denote syphilis—also called "the old rale." Drugs can be called "horse," "nose candy," "high-shooting," "mainlining." AIDS is "the tapout" … This list is already out of date. (see MICKEY MOUSE BAND)

F. Scott Fitzgerald

### "THE JAZZ AGE"

The term is an invention of the press, certain novelists, the movies, show business and popular historians. When F. Scott Fitzgerald published *Tales of the Jazz Age* in 1922, he was accepted as the discoverer, the history-tracing expert on jazz. Actually, Fitzgerald knew little of the real jazz, and imagined any band with a saxophone player was a true jazz band. PAUL WHITEMAN, a popular band leader of ordinary dance music, mostly TIN PAN ALLEY commercial stuff, advertised himself as "The King of Jazz." Whiteman never approved of the true jazz style and kept it out of his band, but did give work to many jazz players in need of jobs, who were warned by "Pops" not to "start swinging the jive."

## JAPANESE JAZZ

**A** people with no modern inventions to their credit—steam engines, electricity, autos, airplanes, radio, T.V., computers, atom crushers—have shown that they can *improve* an outside process, product or art. Examples: the splendid jazz players Sadao Watanabe, alto saxophone; Yoshiaka Masuo, guitar; Toshiko Akiyoshi, piano composer. Most of them have at times played with Chico Hamilton, Gary McFarland ... The late jazz critic Harry Goodwin claimed that the Japanese are too regimented, too respectful to their masters, to be original. "Perhaps in jazz they may break free of binding tradition."

sax time

c. 1948

c. 1950

bass
clarinet

Lapotaire
'32

146

## INSTRUMENTS (cont.)

mostly in the sporting houses. Drums were of parade size at first. The basic drum is a round, hollow shape with stretched skin at both ends. Hit by sticks or a whisk or the hand. Traps include Chinese wooden blocks, cymbals, bass plates, rattles, bells, and gourds. The woods, including the clarinet and saxophone, use a reed. The saxophone didn't arrive until 1920. The oboe and bassoon have a double reed. The strings in common use include the banjo, piano, and guitar. The double bass is the big fellow, usually plucked or slapped. Sometimes there's a cello or violin; there have been fine jazz violinists, and at one time the college boys' favorite, the ukulele. Since its start, many many other instruments—electric or not, new or old—have been added to jazz. Marimbas, xylophones, vibraharps. It still depends on the artists rather than the tools to sound right. (see THE JAZZ BAND)

## INSTRUMENTS

There is no standard set of instruments that are a must for playing jazz. Unlike classical music, early jazz did not include a composer's listing of what the music was to be played with. There usually was no written version of the music, since composers rarely could set down musical scores. Jefferson's slaves, he noted, played "the benjar" (banjo). Early there were flutes, private harps, fiddles, drums for church and work songs. And tunes to dance to, usually barefoot. After the Civil War, when army bands' instruments often ended up in pawn shops, blacks acquired them. Horns were cornets, trumpets, trombones, a French horn. Their sounds come from air vibration in coiled tubes controlled by the lips and valves, which change the tones of the volumes of air. The trombone is controlled by movable slides. Mutes, often a derby hat, fit into or over the bell-ends, and are used to change sounds. The piano was found

death of a jazz man

1982

# H

## HOOCH

It was also called booze, the sauce, panther piss, tiger sweat, whisky and gin, of course. It was the major cause of death among men and women in the jazz world, with drugs often a far second. It kept one warm, or seemed to. It was a barrier against the blues: those times when Old Man Trouble, lost love and a hovering white world were ready to dump on you. It was cheap and often dreadful stuff, brewed in some bathtub, distilled from any mixture that could be made into alcohol. "Jake" was a form of liquor that brought the deep six, killed the use of one's limbs, even blindness. Yet any mixture that could numb the misery of the world, blot out the enemies of existence, was welcome. It cut the pangs of hunger, no place to sleep, the memory of a two-timing woman and, most of all, the sounds of jazz that escaped you, the notes your talent would never reach ... One more for the road ... Only there ain't no road.

# H

## BILLIE "LADY DAY" HOLIDAY (ELEANOR GOUGH) (1915-1959)

A genius of jazz singing, a tragic life marked Billie's destiny. Her early life was a mess of family problems. By 1928, in New York, she was a prostitute and was in jail for four months. But she had an amazing voice, and in Harlem she sang at the Log Cabin Club for coins, but soon other clubs began to pay her. The critic John Hammond heard her and spoke to BENNY GOODMAN about her—she recorded with him, with LESTER YOUNG, DUKE ELLINGTON, also COUNT BASIE. She was at her best at CAFE SOCIETY, but her personal life was still a mess. Drugs, drink led to a Federal Reformatory. Her way with a song was amazing; enriched, touching. Arrested again, she died in a hospital at the age of 44.

1951

# H

## EARL "FATHA" HINES (1905-  )

Like many more jazzmen than one would expect, Hines had a good musical education and was backed by a musical family. He was born in Pittsburgh. Found as a young talent by Lois Deppe, he toured with her and then set up in Chicago, where he played with LOUIS ARMSTRONG, SIDNEY BECHET and JOHNNY DODDS. His piano solo recordings made him famous in jazz circles, and he soon had a big band of his own. He was daring, and hired such young stallions as CHARLIE PARKER and DIZZY GILLESPIE. His piano style was amazing—some called it "the piano trumpet." He dared the 88 keys of the piano to go beyond the old disciplines of bass and treble tones. There is an RCA recording, *The Fatha Jumps,* that excites in the pleasure of his style. His playing of DUKE ELLINGTON may even surpass the master.

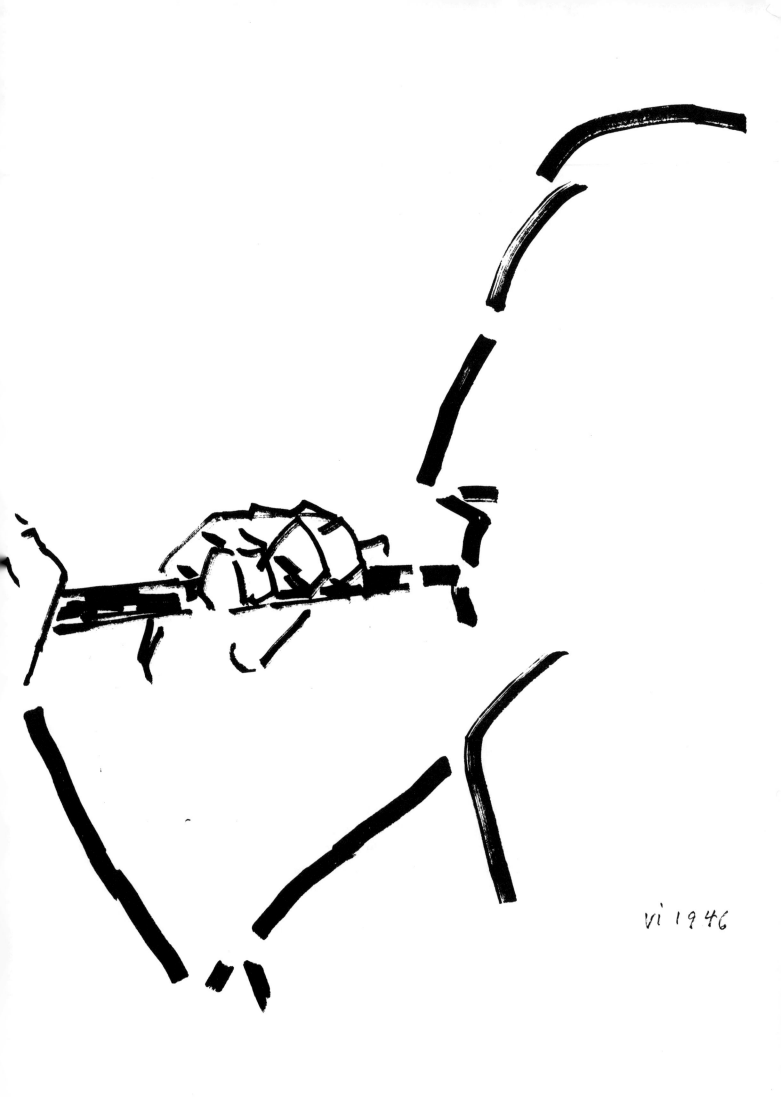

vi 1946

# H

## WOODY HERMAN (1913-1988)

Born in the Midwest, as a boy he appeared in vaudeville shows, he took up the saxophone in high school, and by 1933 was in Chicago playing in the bands of Gus Arnheim and Harry Sosnik. Later he recorded for Decca with Isham Jones as tenor sax and on the clarinet. *The Woody Herman Orchestra* played fine Dixieland, blues and modern arrangements of ELLINGTON. Soon he was one of the masters of modern jazz, and was into classical SWING. His recordings of "Lemon Drop," "Early Autumn," "Four Brothers," and "More Moon" are among the most popular of their period. In 1956, with a new band, he was in Las Vegas. His clarinet rivaled GOODMAN's. As times changed, after many years at the top, he fell from sight and was discovered living in poverty in 1986. Friends rallied and eased his condition. But he was in poor health. His past was recalled, and he had a short return to fame before he died.

# H

## *JAMES FLETCHER HENDERSON* (1898-1952)

**A** serious student of chemistry in Atlanta, he didn't take to music as a profession until he got to New York City in 1920. He took whatever musical job was around, and played piano for Bessie Smith and MA RAINEY. Soon he had a pop band that was taking on the real jazz. He had the first BIG BAND seating sixteen players. In 1939, Henderson gave up his band to play with BENNY GOODMAN, for whom he'd done some arranging. His career ended in 1950 when he had a stroke, and he died two years later. His arranging was splendid, most thought it better than his piano playing. He helped set the standard for the SWING band style. A valid warrior for the best of jazz.

1928

# H

## THE HARLEM RENAISSANCE

It was called the Harlem Renaissance, the 1920s in which blacks from Africa, the West Indies and the United States mingled their ideas and talents in a romantic, creative, productive way. They were among the first, if not the first, to see jazz as an original American art form. The sound of the music mingled for them with thousands of blacks taking Sunday strolls on Seventh Avenue. The artistic and intellectual fervor during the Renaissance, when singer-actor Paul Robeson, black nationalist Marcus Garvey, scholar Alaine Locke and authors Langston Hughes and Zora Neale Hurston were forces of black pride. Ironically, for the average person only the jazz survived; the poems, the plays, and the paintings had little popular memory.

# H

## HARLEM

"Harlem is a black city," Ethel Waters once observed, "entirely surrounded by a bigger city called New York." George Washington fought the British here, and once it was a residential district of well-off whites. Today it's home to a million black people, "where you go and maybe there is room for you." The heart of Harlem is 131st Street and Seventh Avenue, and as it fans out is where jazz was first established around the time of the First World War. It came from out of the south, but in Harlem it had its clubs and stage shows, its joys and its tragedies: housewives shopping, and kids on one skate sliding by; busy poolrooms, sellers of soul food and barbecued meat. Here the COTTON CLUB once flourished, JOSEPHINE BAKER charlestoned, black poets and prophets preached, pious blacks had storefront churches, and DUKE ELLINGTON broadcast the first jazz on radio, nationally. Jazz was the password at the Performers and Entertainers Club, The Hoofers Club, The Lafayette Theater and Tabbs Restaurant, the Tree of Hope, where one could buy "gauge," and the Bandbox where one hoped to pick up a gig. The ofaginzys (whites) came to hear "Minnie the Moocher." This was also the Harlem of rent parties, relief checks, yard toilets, cold-water flats. The jazz stars are gone now, replaced by pushers of crack.

# H

## *LIL HARDIN* (1902?-1971)

**A** well-educated music student, she took to the piano and after leaving Fisk University played in Chicago with JELLY ROLL MORTON. Soon she was with KING OLIVER. In 1922, LOUIS ARMSTRONG came upriver to join Oliver; he and Lil liked each other's style and were married in 1924. Louie may or may not have had a wife, Daisy, in New Orleans. Lil civilized Louie, got him to study a text of cornet solos and take lessons on the European style of handling a horn. Lil was a remarkable musical talent, and did much for the Oliver band. She toured with the group to California, played with Louie and a group at the Dreamland Café and was at the piano for the recordings of Armstrong's *Hot Five, Lil's Hot Shots* and JOHNNY DODDS' *New Orleans Wanderers.* She toured England and France and played with SIDNEY BECHET. One of the few great early women jazz figures who was not a singer.

"Don't shake my tree!"

longstreet

# H

## HALLS OF FAME

Announced for the early 1990s, an International Jazz Hall of Fame is scheduled to be built in Kansas City, Missouri, the hometown of such jazz greats as COUNT BASIE and CHARLIE PARKER. The announcement was made by DIZZY GILLESPIE, the Hall of Fame's national chairman. The $4.8 million project will consist of existing structures and new construction at the site that was home to many 24-hour-a-day jazz clubs in the late 20s. It will include the Count Basie Academy of Performing Arts, the Mahalia Jackson Academy of Gospel Music and the Parker-Gillespie Institute of Jazz Masters. In New Brunswick, New Jersey, Rutgers University's Institute of Jazz Studies and the New Jersey Jazz Society have recently founded the American Jazz Hall of Fame, and are in the midst of renovating part of the city's cultural center facilities to house the plaques of the Hall of Fame's growing membership, a museum of jazz memorabilia and a collection of audio and video tapes.

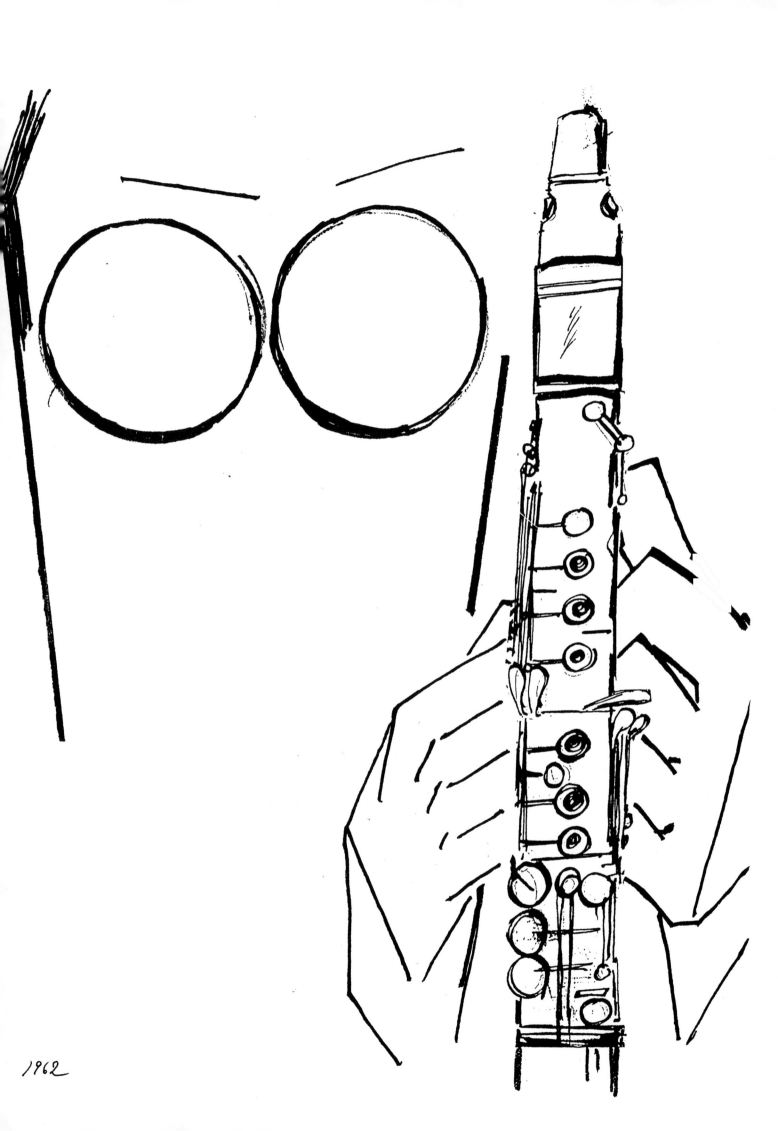

1962

*G*

## BENNY GOODMAN (1909-1986)

Born in Chicago, his interest and skill on the clarinet never wavered. At the age of ten, he was playing in synagogues. At sixteen, he was a professional with a popular band, Ben Pollack's group. He moved around and began to record; worked on stage, in radio, made film shorts. In 1934, he had his own band; toured the nation and reached its height in public appearances at Los Angeles's Palomar Ballroom. By 1938, he was "the King of Swing," with a concert in Carnegie Hall. In Hollywood he was featured in major films: *The Big Broadcast, Hollywood Hotel, Stage Door Canteen.* He composed "Stompin' at the Savoy," "Swingtime in the Rockies." His clarinet style remained that of a master, a man with imagination.

Lord Street

Monterey '78

*G*

## JOHN BIRKS "DIZZY" GILLESPIE (1917-   )

He was born as John Birks Gillespie, but no one seems to remember that. His father was a band musician, so Dizzy played all the instruments, settled on the trombone as a boy—soon went over to the trumpet to win music scholarships. By 1935, he was picking up band jobs and fell under the spell of ROY ELDRIDGE—whom he later replaced with Teddy Hill's band in New York City. He was in Europe playing jazz, and came back to join CAB CALLOWAY. In 1945, he was back in New York at Minton's Playhouse forming bands of BOP players with CHARLIE PARKER. They did *Jazz at Massey Hall* together, and Dizzy showed interest in Afro-Cuban drummers. A man with a fey sense of humor, one never knew which way he would turn. Even had his personal record label: *Dee Gee.* Modern jazz owes a great deal to Dizzy Gillespie, a brainy man, an adventurer. His brassy solos are in a class by themselves.

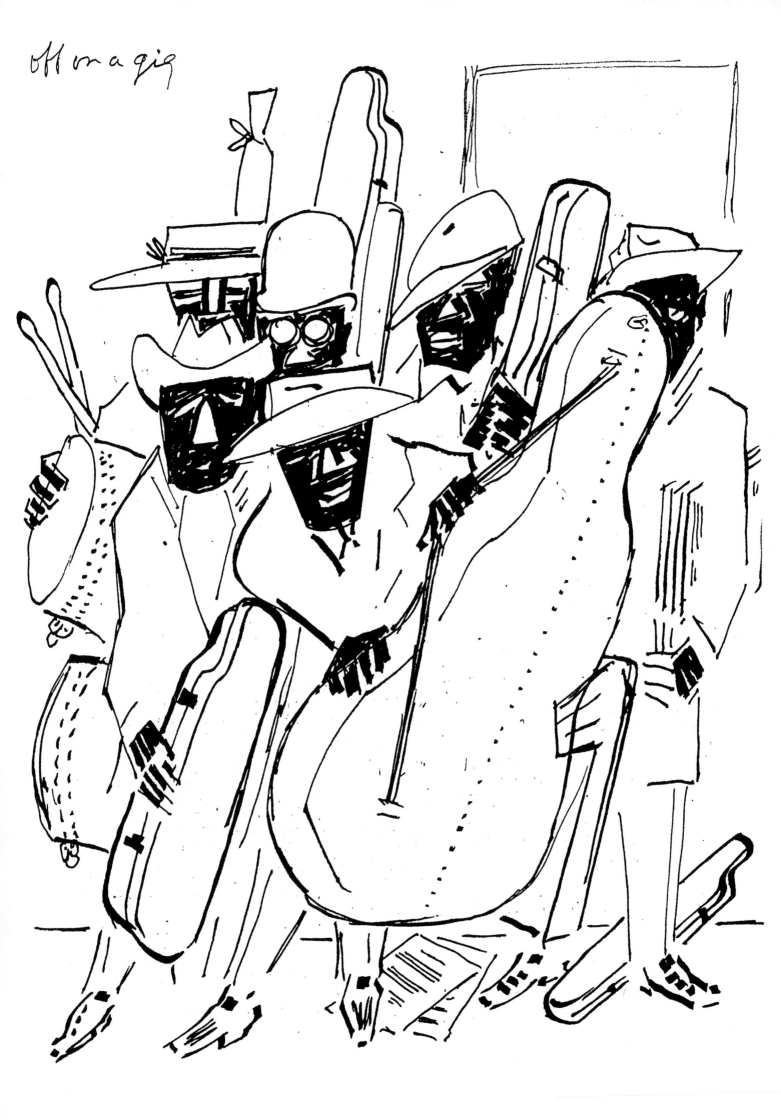

# *G*

## *THE GIG*

Louis armstrong insisted the word "gig" is for a pickup playing date; came from a sort of carriage that in the early days of jazz would carry a couple of jazzmen out to some country dance in need of musicians to fill in for those who had not shown up. No one is sure if that is the correct answer. But every singer, dancer, player knows what it means; to "hunt a gig," "play a gig." A gig is any kind of a musical job—usually of short duration, a one-nighter, a weekend, or to finish the heel of a season. The true tragic drama in the life of a jazz player is that desperate last moment when shoe leather is thin, rent is overdue and jobs seem filled—then there must be just *one* gig left. Lord, let it be for me.

# G

**STAN GETZ** (1927-     )

Born in Philadelphia, a graduate of the James Monroe High School, he was soon playing in the New York All-City Orchestra. He seemed safe as a classical musician. But by 1944, he was playing with STAN KENTON, JIMMY DORSEY and BENNY GOODMAN, and later with WOODY HERMAN.. A master of the tenor saxophone, Stan appeared in the movie *The Benny Goodman Story* and with such groups as *The Metronome All Stars.* A master of BOP riffs, he has worked with GILLESPIE and PARKER, been a major voice on the international jazz scene, and won a Grammy Award.

*G*

## *GEORGE GERSHWIN* (1898-1937)

**H**e belongs in the jazz story, not as a pure jazzman, but as a sort of transmission belt between the real jazz and the popular standards on which some of the jazz idiom rubbed off. Without trying to pinpoint just where he fits in, Gershwin was a musical talent. As a teenager he was already a TIN PAN ALLEY song plugger, and aware of the new kind of music in the air. He wrote "Swanee" but later tried seriously to suggest that the roots of jazz could be woven into American music. In 1924, PAUL WHITEMAN, never a true jazzman, commissioned Gershwin to compose his "Rhapsody In Blue" for a concert at Aeolian Hall in New York City. Certainly it contained jazz themes, but more Gershwin than New Orleans. He later wrote a folk opera, *Porgy and Bess,* and some marvelous and popular music that arrangers have brought over into the jazz tradition. When ELLINGTON was told he was "the black Gershwin," he replied, "No, Gershwin is the white Ellington."

c. 1949

# F

## FUSION

Rock music of course came out of rock 'n' roll and it had its heroes and its phonies, its martyrs and its promoters. It had a following among some jazz voices and players, those who wanted to move beyond BOP and work in some rock. It took the name "rock-fusion-jazz" or "jazz-rock-fusion." Singers Al Jarreau, Michael Franks, a piano man like David Frishberg, have written some of its music. Sometimes it has a touch of swing, often it tastes of commercial pop. The lyrics can be avant garde or banal, and to some it isn't jazz.

# F

## FUNK

Funk is also by some called "hard BOP," as pushed by the Horace Silver quintet in 1956. With blue roots and funky sound using a heartfelt melodic line. The harmony was good and when a group like "Cannonball" Adderley's played funk—hard bop—it was brisk, fun music, simple, it never got tangled up. Some of their most popular music was "This Here" and of course "Dat Dere" and "Sack o' Woe." By the time the 1960s had come around, bop, be-bop, hard bop, COOL JAZZ and funk had had their day. Yet bop remains as a major strain in all good jazz; a tough survivor.

Verve Records - 1956

# F

## *ELLA FITZGERALD* (1918-    )

**A**n orphan, she came to live with an aunt in New York City, where she sang in amateur contests. From the *Harlem Amateur Hour,* Chick Webb hired her for his big band. In the 1930s they were at the Savoy (Webb was co-author of "Stompin' at the Savoy.") In 1935, she recorded "A Tisket, A Tasket." When Webb died, she took over the band. But soon she was the soloist with many groups, even did pop recordings. She appeared in films and in Las Vegas, toured the world, including Asia and South America. Bothered with eye trouble, she retired for some years, but with sight improved she was back as a soloist. She never pressed a song—her approach is subtle, clear, never cold. There is class to her singing, and the tone of a great talent.

Group Jazz

# F

## 52nd STREET

From the 30s to the 50s, "52nd Street" meant clubs featuring the newest jazz sounds and the hottest voices: ART TATUM, Nat King Cole, BILLIE HOLIDAY, even Doris Day before she went to Hollywood to train to be a virgin. The best-known clubs on the streets between Fifth and Sixth Avenues were Kelly's Stable, Down Beat, the Onyx, Jimmy Ryan's, Hickory House, the Deuces. The food and drink may have been so-so, but the jazz was usually the best that could be heard.

LE JAZZ HOT
CLUB·FRANCE

Paris
Soostrey 28

# E

## EUROPE'S FIRST JAZZ

RAGTIME got to Europe early in the new century. MINSTREL SHOWS played there with the cakewalk, and Irene and Vernon Castle introduced the Bunny Hug, but it was Americans in World War I who had created several "Negro Army Bands." One was led by James Reese Europe, later known to jazz as Jim Europe. A jazz pianist in the army, he played Sousa and George M. Cohan. After the war he stayed on in France and put jazz groups together. Jim Europe found he could make a living in France. In 1919, Will Cook's *Syncopated Southern Orchestra* was in Paris with SIDNEY BECHET starring for a time. A white group there was *The Original Dixieland Jass.* In 1932, LOUIE ARMSTRONG himself came, and the next year DUKE ELLINGTON was dining at the Ritz to announce: "Love you, dearly." There were many blacks who settled in Paris, played jazz with French or visiting Americans. JOSEPHINE BAKER became "more French than the French."

# E

## EDWARD KENNEDY "DUKE" ELLINGTON
(1899-1974)

They called him "Duke" even when he was a kid because he already showed class. He was born in Washington, D.C., into a well-off family, well educated. In high school he wrote the "Soda Fountain Rag" and began to work with local groups. In 1919, he had his own bands, *The Duke's Serenaders* and the *Washingtonians*. By 1923, he was at New York's Hollywood Club. Fame came when he went to Harlem's COTTON CLUB, and onto national radio. His first hit was "Mood Indigo" ... "I Love You Madly," he announced. As a composer, alone or with others, came "It Don't Mean a Thing," "Black and Tan Fantasy," "The Mooch." He toured the U.S.A., Europe. He produced "Take The 'A' Train," "Chelsea Bridge," "A Drum Is a Woman." In 1943, New York held a Duke Ellington Week. His orchestra was his monument. His music national treasures.

1971

# E

## *ROY ELDRIDGE* (1911-1989)

A rough, splendid, brassy, swinging trumpet player—
DIZZY'S style took a lot from him, as did other young horn
men. He was playing drums aged six, the trumpet at
eleven. At sixteen touring with his own band, then working tent shows, carnivals. In 1936, he was with FLETCHER
HENDERSON and later a soloist for Artie Shaw and GENE
KRUPA. He was in Paris with BENNY GOODMAN, and stayed
over there for a time. ELLA FITZGERALD used him for
recordings. His playing was solid and he remained sure
of himself and his style; with his own bands or taking
solos with other groups.

Longstreet
Chicago '48

# D

## JIMMY DORSEY (1904-1957)
## TOMMY DORSEY (1905-1956)

One has to dig through the stories of the wild Irish battling brothers to get to the core of their great value as musicians. Their father was a bandleader who played the cornet. Jimmy took to the clarinet and alto saxophone, played in his father's brass band, and then with the *Scranton Sirens* and Jean Goldkette. At eighteen there was the *Dorsey Novelty* band. He also played with PAUL WHITEMAN and RED NICHOLS. Tommy Dorsey took to the trombone; he also played in his father's band and with the *Scranton Sirens*, then went over to the *California Ramblers.* He did pop music with Vincent Lopez, Ted Lewis, and Rudi Vallee. Later he played with pure jazzmen: BIX, *The Goofus Five*, RED NICHOLS. By 1934, there was *The Dorsey Brothers Orchestra*. Many jazz stars from Max Kaminsky to Bud Freeman, Buddy Rich, and Buddy Berigan worked with the Dorseys. The Dorsey versions of popular tunes they turned into splendid music included "I'm Getting Sentimental Over You," "Smoke Gets in Your Eyes," "On the Sunny Side of the Street." Then the stories of the battling Dorseys started, and Tommy soon had his own band. The brothers were personalities and in 1947 there was the movie *The Fabulous Dorseys,* proving they were great jazzmen and poor actors. The brothers died within a year of each other, still battling, people said.

# D

**JOHNNY DODDS** (1892-1940)

He came up with the New Orleans school of clarinet jazz. Born when it was starting to come together, he worked with Kid Ory, LOUIS ARMSTRONG and then with KING OLIVER—the Hall of Fame of early jazz. He liked Chicago—had his own bands and much to show the white jazz players what a warm casual style one could get from a clarinet. He worked with Louis Armstrong on his *Hot Five* and *Hot Seven* records. When the Depression came, he drove a taxi between gigs. He was playing in 1940 when he sounded his last note.

1946

# D

## DIXIELAND JAZZ

Early on, this term, now used loosely, was applied to white jazzmen or bands, and included Papa Jack Laine, an alto horn player, Leon Rappalo on clarinet and Nick La Rocca on cornet. The Dixieland bands embraced *Sam Morgan's Jazz Band,* Louis Drumaine's *Jazzola Eight,* Tony Parenti's *Famous Melody Boys*. The first recorded band, in 1917, was *The Original Dixieland Jazz Band*. Early jazz players toured with shows, played in the pit of vaudeville houses, under BURLESQUE theater runways, even tent shows. So jazz penetrated the heartland and the tank towns and the gas-lit variety houses turning to electric lights, and something called "the movies" ... All in an odor of stage makeup, insect spray and popcorn; the curtain would go up in over a thousand American towns to the sound of ragtime and jazz from the orchestras.

# D

## DISC JOCKEY

It was radio in the mid-1920s that first brought jazz to the attention of the American (usually counted as "average") starting with DUKE ELLINGTON's broadcasts from Harlem's COTTON CLUB. Soon broadcasting of records over the air became popular and the often glib, fast-talking men who changed the records filled in with chitchat, usually called "hip." These became the disc jockeys. Today they broadcast a mixture of rock 'n' roll, country, pop, and jazz. Often disc jockeys have a cult following.

Longstreet
1954

# D

## *MILES DAVIS* (1926-    )

He was the son of a well-off dentist, and so a patient of his father's traded work on his teeth for lessons on the trumpet for Miles. He played with local bands as a teenager and he also heard the first strains of BOP, and met PARKER and GILLESPIE. His parents insisted he go to the Juilliard School of Music in New York but he spent more time on 52ND STREET with the bop people. He worked with Parker, COLEMAN, BENNY CARTER. By 1949, he had his own group, playing the trombone, even piano, drums and the bass, and recording *Birth of THE COOL*. He played at the Paris Jazz Festival, and was also hooked on heroin. Some say Miles kicked the habit in time. At the NEWPORT JAZZ FESTIVAL of 1955, he was such a sensation that Columbia signed him to record. His quintet was an astonishing group and became the most important of all the small groups ever to appear in jazz. With Gil Evans he made a whole series of remarkable recordings, beginning with *Miles Ahead*. He went on to become one of the great milestones of advanced music. Bringing in Latin-American tones and music from India to a career that seems never-ending.

# D

## DANCING TO JAZZ

Various dances came and went; jitterbugging, strutting continued—the shimmy, dipsy doodle, boogie-woogie and always tap steps; every little change in a step gave it a new name, most now forgotten; various wriggles and stomps had their moments. In New York, the Savoy and Connie's Inn were places to see the newest trendsetters' fancy footwork. "Ten Cents a Dance" joints, like Roseland, mixed jazz and popular music, and a few jazz men of merit, when times were hard, played there, but not unless the wolf was really at the door. The customers were more for the clutch than the classics.

## THE COTTON CLUB

Legend covered the Cotton Club, and a bad movie recently gave it the wrong color. The real Cotton Club was created by white gangsters for white after-theater guests, on the corner of 142nd Street and Lenox Avenue in Harlem. In this place it existed, with some of the most exciting bands, from 1923 to 1936. Its first great hit was DUKE ELLINGTON, a rising young genius, who did radio broadcasts from the place and helped jazz go national, to places and people that never knew a night club. He was followed by the whirling CAB CALLOWAY. Appearing at the Cotton Club were Bill Robinson tapping, Ethel Waters, Lena Horne singing, LOUIS ARMSTRONG trumpeting and Buck and Bubbles dancing. In 1936, the Cotton Club moved to off Times Square, with CAFE SOCIETY taking it up, and it became so popular it turned away business. Dorothy Dandridge was one of its stars. But high costs and the changing tastes of thrillseekers caused its last notes to sound in 1940.

*C*

## COOL JAZZ

Cool jazz was really one way of playing BOP—a variation that came from MILES DAVIS, who added French horn and tuba to his band, kept the music poetic and light, not improvised; it was arranged. Those who saw it as an art form, beyond dance or popular entertainment, made a cult of cool jazz—mostly the serious jazz musicians. LENNIE TRISTANO reached even higher, his cool was the coolest. It was called highbrow, avant garde. They reached for emotional depth and the mind of the listener. They often avoided inflections, talked of fugues. They were players of carefully studied and arranged music. GERRY MULLIGAN was an early convert.

## L

### JOHN "TRANE" COLTRANE (1926-1967)

**A**mong the mystics found in the jazz people, John Coltrane was the deepest, at times into the occult. In a North Carolina high school he played an alto horn, then went to the clarinet and then to the saxophone. In Philadelphia he was at the Ornstein Music School. In 1949, he was with GILLESPIE's big band, but went on to study music at the Granoff School. By 1955, he was with MILES DAVIS and with THELONIOUS MONK, but always remained his own man. He was known as a great jazz soloist, his style "sheets of sound." There also appeared a great interest in Eastern godheads and the India sounds in his playing. He called an album *Giant Steps*. The "new thing," as it was called, was very personal in his style, often made up of four-note motifs. His spiritual side was often over-balanced by the physical. He was a heavy user of heroin and a gross eater; he grew heavy, which did not aid his continued bad health. His after-bop music of the late 1950s and its continued impressive progress contained Western and Eastern music mixed with ease. He distrusted doctors, ignored strange pains, but he could still go from low to three octaves higher. At last taken to a hospital, he died of complications and a diseased liver.

*C*

## ORNETTE COLEMAN (1930-    )

Many think him to be "the greatest saxophone player since CHARLIE PARKER." Born in Fort Worth, self-taught, he began as an ordinary bandplayer. Some even thought him a bad one, showing little talent. He was often fired from a gig. In 1950, he was on the West Coast where he met the trumpet player Don Cherry. They formed a strong friendship that seemed to alert their playing. They recorded with Contemporary Records and soon they were a group that was making modern jazz news. They went to New York to play at the Five Spots and record for Atlantic *The Shape of Jazz to Come.* They were cheered or booed. Coleman was big jazz news. His style was always unorthodox, sometimes hard bop. He began to compose in a style he called "Harmolody." His best-known works may be "Lonely Woman," "Tears Inside," "Ramblin'" and "Una Muy Bonita." He has certainly been at the head of the jazz avant garde of his time.

*C*

## CHICAGO or *JAZZPORT*

The city was destined by history and geography to be the mother of North Central jazz. The United States took over the setting in 1795 from the Indians, and called it Fort Dearborn. The British burned it in 1812. It burned itself down in the Great Chicago Fire of 1871. It was built on mud, on pork, the great railroad hub. By the time of World War I, jazz, or jazz sounds, were heard, and the riverboats and steam cars would soon bring in the needed dance music that the CAPONE clubs and cafés and roadhouses needed: the sound of braying trumpets and the real jazz sessions, the solos of the men around KING OLIVER and those who followed. The white high-school kids like BENNY GOODMAN and BIX BEIDERBECKE listened. The Chicago sound was as popular as bootlegging. (see THE WOLVERINES)

Harlem vii 26

*C*

## THE CHARLESTON

It began as a craze, then became a symbol of the Twenties. Even some of the middle-aged took it up, or tried. It first appeared in Harlem in the show *Liza*, in 1922, and then in the theater of *Running Wild.* It consisted of uninhibited glee, flinging one's limbs about and then bringing the knees together and pulling them apart. Each group tried out its own trimmings. Its greatest popularity came when the movies took it up as expressing "wild youth." Featuring Ginger Rogers, Joan Crawford, and George Raft. It was the first of the black dances to move over into white territory, and Charleston Contests swept the nation. It lasted longer than most dance crazes. JOSEPHINE BAKER introduced it to Europe, and her long-legged frenzy made her the idol of Paris.

*C*

**BENNY CARTER** (1907-    )

He came from a family of musicians, was born in New York City. He played early the C-melody and the alto saxophone, also sometimes the trumpet. In 1933, he had his own band, including TEDDY WILSON. He was in Paris in 1935 with Willie Lewis, and stayed abroad for three years. While living in California, he made some of his best recordings, composed and created film scores; worked for Alfred Hitchcock and singers SARAH VAUGHAN, Pearl Bailey, Ray Charles. He worked in many fields of jazz; arranging, composing, at the saxophone, the trumpet. Benny Carter is the man-of-all-jazz. Even lecturing on the subject in universities.

Longstreet
iv '27

*C*

## AL CAPONE  (1899-1947)

**S**ome called Capone "the patron saint of CHICAGO jazz."
He owned or controlled many of the night clubs, roadhouses and dance halls, and gave work to the jazzmen
and -women in need of places to perform. He himself
liked grand opera, but knew what the public wanted ...
The best-known night clubs, maybe controlled by
Capone or maybe not, were the Royal Gardens, the
Plantation Café, Dreamland, the Pekin Café, the Friars
Inn. Going down State Street from the Loop were the
sporting house sections in which Capone had an interest, around 22nd Street. There would be jazzmen shiver-
ing in the cold lake breeze, looking for a gig among the
cold-water flats and the speakeasies. There was the
Entertainers Cabaret at which EARL HINES played a push-
around piano. Chicago's posh places were Pony Moore's
and the famous Everleigh Club, where there was often
good jazz. This sketch of him was done in ten seconds
while he passed through a hotel lobby.

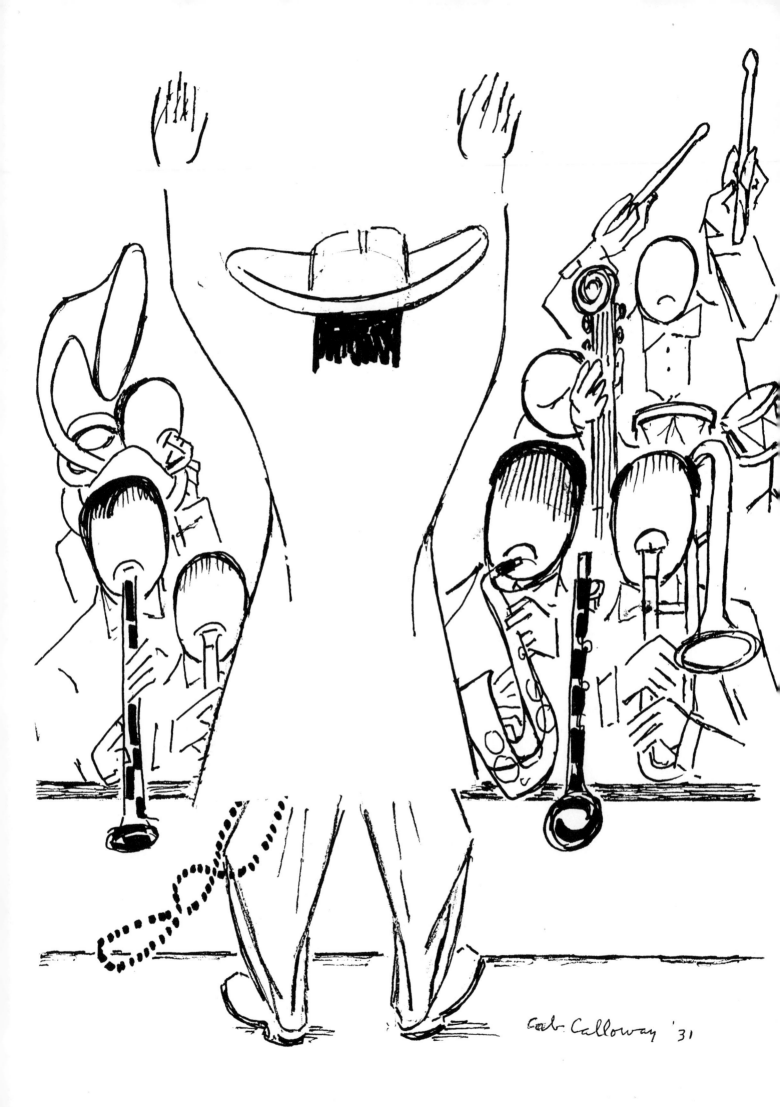

*C*

### *CABELL "CAB" CALLOWAY* (1907-　)

**S**ome have been put off by Cab's prancing, whirling clowning as a bandleader, but his roots were set in early jazz; behind his jiving movements, his bands could produce a solid jazz style. He began as a singer and dancer, and came to fame with his chanting of his trademark, "Minnie the Moocher," the tale of a coke-sniffing frail. In 1929, he was with the band at the Savoy Ballroom; the group followed DUKE ELLINGTON into the COTTON CLUB, where "Minnie" and Cab's antics on the bandstand brought him fame. He appeared in films, *The Big Broadcast*, *Stormy Weather,* and with Al Jolson in *The Singing Kid.* He also played the character Sportin' Life in GERSHWIN's opera *Porgy and Bess.*

*C*

## *CAFE SOCIETY*

Café Society, a jazz club, was opened by Barney Josephson at 2 Sheridan Square in New York, December 1938. He said: "I wanted a club where blacks and whites worked together behind the footlights and sat together out front. There wasn't, so far as I know, a place like it in New York or in the whole country." Although from the earliest days of jazz, black musicians played for white audiences, few nightclubs permitted blacks and whites to mix in the audience. Josephson's café was the first nightclub in a white neighborhood to welcome customers of all races. He had no musical background; he had worked in shoe stores. For the next decade, Café Society and Café Society Uptown, which Josephson opened two years later on East 58th Street, were producing a long list of singers, comedians, and jazz musicians, including BILLIE HOLIDAY, who sang in the opening show in 1938 and remained there nine months. In 1947, Mr. Josephson's brother Leon, an avowed Communist, was subpoenaed by the House Committee on Un-American Activities. Barney Josephson was attacked by columnists Westbrook Pegler and Walter Winchell, and business at the two clubs dropped. He hung on for a year until, losing $90,000, he sold both clubs.

1935

# B

## BURLESQUE SHOW JAZZ

The American burlesque show came over as English music hall entertainment, but once here soon took on a more raucous, frontier tone. It needed more than the melodies of RAGTIME—and with the bringing in of TIN PAN ALLEY sound, jazz was found to be very useful for the climax of the gamey blackouts, the timing of the actions of the strippers and the right sounds for the bumps and grinds of an *artiste* of body action—each grind, jerk and twist to be set in place by the fast reaction of the drummer and the bray of trumpets as they announced the victory of outlaw anatomy over discarded costume.

# B

## BOURBON STREET

The street in NEW ORLEANS is both a legend and a fact. Here a great deal of the early New Orleans style was played, and the sound of jazz was always heard on this not too impressive street. Its buildings were never grand, its facades shabby, and it was given to bars and cafés. But it has retained some of its past, catering to tourists and the fans of the old classic jazz. Here for the cost of a couple of beers, you can sit and listen to old jazzmen on a platform playing what some think is the jazz as BUDDY BOLDEN, KING OLIVER, and Kid Ory blew it out. Or so it's claimed. The old horn players may not have known LOUIS ARMSTRONG, or played in the sporting houses in the days of Nell Kimball, as they claim; but their sound is the real thing.

# B

## BOP CITY

The downtowns of the big cities in the 50s and 60s were often called Bop City, dominated by the sound of crowds, loudspeakers of radio shops, street music, dance studios, music studios. Dominated too by bars with a honky-tonk piano, pawnshops, soul-food dives, hoofer clubs, slock bargains. And people: working girls and tarts, gig hunters, sidewalk salesmen and sandwich men, hairdressers, curb concerts and Honest Harry's Used Cars. The sound was deafening. Newsboys, shine offers and jazz recordings, rock 'n' roll, country and blue grass, the last of the street cars, and the downtown traffic. In some doorways, offers of "hot" fur coats, recordings and "Swiss" watches, while unemployed jazz-men stood around with their instruments hoping for rumors of a job.

1945

Longstreet

# B

## BOP, BE-POP

You could play at bop and not think about it, but the Columbus, the Daniel Boone of bop, was CHARLIE PARKER, the greatest modern innovator in jazz; a virtuoso saxophone man and already a legend. He came out of Kansas City in 1939 with his own unique style. He attracted the young horn player DIZZY GILLESPIE, and also the drummer Kenny Clarke. Between them, Bop was born. Oddly rhythmic, flexible music, the jazzmen saw it as free from the overpolished, oversweet music the BIG BANDS insisted they play. There were bop recordings on the market by 1944. Bop stretches harmony beyond old disciplines—uses half-stops, versatile, accenting measures, crowding extra notes, even added melodies from other songs. To some it lacked melody.

# B

## BOOGIE-WOOGIE

STRIDE music, as it progressed, changed into another piano style called boogie-woogie, while still retaining some connection with RAGTIME. Bass and treble played against each other—and some found it not as smooth as what had preceded it. It introduced the influence of the GUITAR and rough-house saloon piano, with more of a touch of the blues. A rolling bass and intimate treble were its trademark. EARL "FATHA" HINES was one of its masters, later came Art Hodes, TEDDY WILSON, ART TATUM.

PHOTO: C 1900

# B

## CHARLES "BUDDY" BOLDEN ("KING")
(1868?-1931)

He is not an invented legend—only a few years ago you could touch people who had known him. To many he is the first master of jazz at its birth. No true photograph of him is known, and he made no recordings. By 1893, he was the macho master of black New Orleans; a popular barber, a mighty horn player in street parades and on the platform at Persevance Hall, Tin Type Hall. Jass, or jazz, wasn't respectable to church-going blacks, and why did Buddy Bolden play his horn that new way and the players copy him? When his music caught on, and his style, poor Buddy went crazy during a street parade. In 1907, they locked him up in the East Louisiana State Hospital—the nut farm. They took away his horn and gave him the white coat of a barber. He cut hair until 1931. Or was being a sporting barber just another part of his legend?

# B

## THE BLUES

The ROOTS of the blues lie in the spirituals, the laments of jail and work songs. They came to jazz through the great singers, MA RAINEY, "Mother of the Blues," Bessie Smith, and BILLIE HOLIDAY, who made the songs over to their own phrasing and conception. The blues expressed loss of lovers, despair at life's burdens, and hope as the great sin. It's in Bessie Smith's recordings of "Empty Bed Blues," in Billie Holiday's "Gloomy Sunday." White singers like Libbie Holman and Helen Morgan had their own version of the blues. While most of the best blues singers have been women, there have been men, often called "Blues Shouters," with strong voices and firm phrasing, men like Big Joe Turner, Jimmy Rushing, and Ray Charles.

# B

## BLUE MOVIES

**P**orno or erotic filmmakers were outside the law and often pirated jazz recordings as background music to the foreground action. The music was usually mutilated, chopped and often badly rerecorded. Erotic movies that claimed art-house patrons usually had scores written for them, also strongly slanted to jazz.

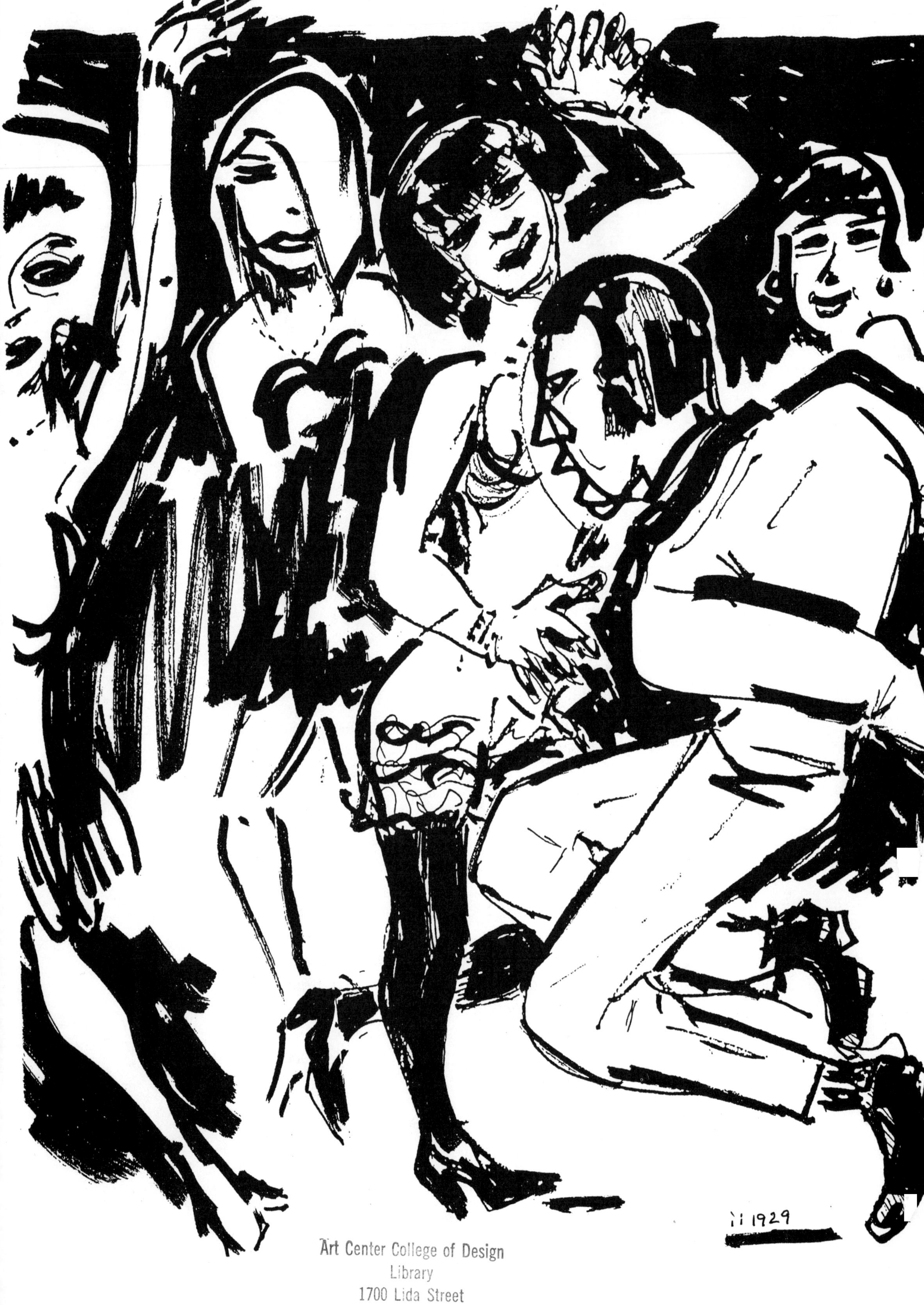
1929

# B

## THE BLACK BOTTOM

In contrast to the CHARLESTON, the Black Bottom took over only for a while. It consisted of hopping forward and then hopping back and, in between, slapping oneself on the behind ... Its roots were said to be in black plantation folk carrying on. Some hints of it were in New York by 1919, but it was in 1924 that it clicked in a Harlem show called *Dinah.* Soon it moved to Broadway in George White's *Scandals of 1926*. Black dancers taught it to Ann Pennington, who got too much credit for it. The young, night-clubbing society took it up and the sound of slapped rears was soon heard in the best places, in the nation's ballrooms and at college proms, if the chaperone did not frown on it.

MAY 1952

# B

## BIG BANDS

You can't separate SWING from the era of the big bands. What had begun as nine-, even ten-piece bands, by swing time became a sixteen-piece orchestra. There was *hot* swing and *sweet* swing—large brass and reed sections with popular male and female vocalists. They had improved tone, and jazz never sounded such powerful rhythms. If GOODMAN and ELLINGTON stood out, other leaders also were very popular and very impressive. BENNY CARTER, Don Redman, Jimmy Lunceford, Harry James, WOODY HERMAN, COUNT BASIE. The big bands toured and toured. Never again would there be such a phenomenon.

# B

## THE BIG APPLE

**N**o one knows who first called New York City "The Big Apple." Most jazz historians agree it was the blacks who played jazz and began to arrive in HARLEM in great numbers when we entered World War I. It was heard as "the city called a big apple" early in the 1920s, but does not seem to have appeared in print until 1956 (in my book *The Real Jazz, New and Old,* Univ. of Louisiana Press). To the jazz player and the people of Harlem, "The Big Apple" is the city of New York: shiny, pretty on the outside, but what's inside? Hope? Misery? Joy? Death?

with Whiteman - 1929

# B

### LEON "BIX" BEIDERBECKE (1903-1931)

One of the first great white jazz men, self taught, he was a horn player who added to jazz much original form. By 1923, he was with THE WOLVERINES, the heroes of early white jazz. He went on to Jean Goldkette's group and to play with the DORSEYS, Eddie Lang and with the PAUL WHITEMAN Orchestra. He composed for the piano, among his best being the great jazz classic "In a Mist." His cornet style was rich and true. He died of pneumonia and drink.

1947

# B

## *SIDNEY BECHET* (1897-1959)

The grand old angry man of jazz, a clarinetist of power and much original sound. A virtuoso hard to know. He lived a great deal of his life in France, where he perfected his art on the soprano saxophone. He played with DUKE ELLINGTON and JAMES P. JOHNSON. He toured Europe, including the U.S.S.R. By 1931, he had settled in Paris, and in 1958 was featured in the Brussels World's Fair. His playing was unique, his vibrato outstanding. He died in 1959, a proud rebel to the end.

Count Basie
'42

# B

## WILLIAM "COUNT" BASIE (1904-1984)

He came out of Kansas City, via New Jersey and New York. He played drums and piano as a child, also took organ lessons from FATS WALLER. He played in vaudeville and at the theater organ. In 1929, he was with BENNIE MOTEN's group. By 1935, he had his own band with a rhythm section that became famous. The jazz critic, John Hammond, put together an American tour for the orchestra—then there was New York's Savoy Ballroom—later came movies and the making of his best recordings. His bands of 1950 and later showed him at his best. As a piano soloist there is a delight in his smooth style. He composed the popular "One O'Clock Jump" and remained one of the best leaders of jazz bands.

Longstreet
'58

# B

## THE JAZZ BAND

From the beginning, the jazz band began to organize itself into the INSTRUMENTS that, with few changes, have comprised the jazz band to this day. No matter what changes in style come and go, you need rhythm-making tools. Basic are the string bass, the drums (traps and tools), guitar, banjo; piano, cornet, piccolo, clarinet, trumpet, even a tuba. Any three of the above can be a nucleus, and add one of five kinds of popular saxophones; but from the start, someone had a trombone. Oddly, the jazz image, the saxophone, did not come into the band until the 1920s. All bands had soloists to take on the music for a few licks. Singers to batter the lyrics to fit their voices. Later, bands had arrangers to give them a personal style.

# B

## *JOSEPHINE BAKER* (1905-1987)

**A**t sixteen she was a skinny kid with a round head of shiny hair. Out of St. Louis, she was in a Harlem chorus of *Shuffle Along,* but on her own she stepped forward, mugged and danced, carried on, and the audience went wild. She went on to star in *Chocolate Dandies* as a 'wild' specialty dancer. But Paris called her in the early Twenties, and she was there bringing the jazz note, the CHARLESTON, dancing in a costume made only of bananas. Unlike some Americans in Paris who stayed mostly with other Americans, Josephine moved in among the French, married a French count and sang and danced in French shows. She was one of the first black international stars, and took as the motto of her lifestyle the saying of the French Revolutionary leader Danton: "Audacity, again audacity, *always* audacity." America saw her for the last time in 1951, when in need of money for a children's home, although already aging, she toured the nation. The audacity and the great legs were still there. But no bananas!

# A

## ART ENSEMBLE OF CHICAGO

In Chicago, pianist Muhal Richard Abrams formed *The Association for Advancement of Creative Music*, a group "to preserve all forms of jazz: American, Asian, African, European." Interesting, well worth the listening, amusing too, they played various instruments, each artist his own way. Certainly their infusion of all expressions of blended jazz was ambitious. Out of this group, Roscoe Mitchell and others formed the Art Ensemble of Chicago in 1969.

Lonystreet
c. 1952

**LOUIS "SATCHMO" ARMSTRONG** (1900-1971)

**H**aving grown up in poverty, at 13 he acquired a cornet in a Boys' Home band. He matured his talent playing with KING OLIVER's band as well as on Mississippi river boats. In 1922, King Oliver, now in Chicago, sent for Louie. He became a sensation in that city, and married LIL HARDIN. He went on to New York and FLETCHER HENDERSON. He took to the trumpet and was billed as "The World's Greatest Trumpet Player." He formed *Armstrong's Hot Seven*. He refined his style, invented SCAT SINGING. His fame became international. Louie toured the world, made movies. There is a large bronze statue of him on a street in New Orleans.

c. 1935

## AFRICA AND JAZZ

One can argue all night about the significance of African influences on jazz forms. Most historians see jazz as American in form and style, but a few do not. There are Africans who have mastered modern jazz with great skill. There is the Nigerian Fred Coker, trumpet players Hugh Masekela and Mongezi Feza, sax player Dudu Pukwana, drummer Louis Moholo, and pianist Abdullah Ibrahim, primarily South Africans who have played in Europe. Their inspiration to start with was American jazz. All helped to make jazz international.

be-bop. Fats Waller doing the boogie piano, John Coltrane trying to explain to a few of us how Einstein and jazz are really "the same thing."

It is my hope that all this comes through as easy as A B C. It's a new kind of jazz venture, unlike anything I have done before. It's neither a history nor a memoir. Fresher, I think, closer to the basic essence of the music—close-ups—of the people who created and played it. Some dude once estimated that there have been at least 150,000 men and women involved in jazz as players, singers, composers and back-up people. I have picked some of the best and the most popular, also some of the van Goghs of jazz who might have been overlooked. I have tried to include only reproductions from life, or recalled just after the event pictured. Some of the pictures are now in the Library of Congress, the Smithsonian Institution, the National Portrait Gallery, Yale University, Boston University's Mugar Rare Collections Library, the Oakland and Huntsville Museums, the Erdelac Americana Collection, and other public and private collections, and I acknowledge the owners' permission to allow me to include them here.

S.L.

present day, when I am a graying senior citizen, I have tried to capture in my drawings the sound, the color—in slow motion, or sped up—of the world of jazz people. Tried to trap the very smoke and odor of the dives, the tenseness of concerts, the wail of the blues at Harlem rent parties, or a horn player dying in a Chicago cold-water flat.

I felt that if I could capture directly, with ink, pen or brush, the life moments as they were being played out, I would have more than camera-caught folk history, gone beyond just the pictured act of jazz itself. I hoped to capture, with black marks on white paper, this music created by these people, and set down what they looked like, felt and did before they were gone. And most are gone now; new sounds, rock-jazz-fusion is here. For jazz has changed, is changing, will soon be no longer, in person, visible for what it once was. Can my sketchbooks survive? That is one more reason for making this book. To catch, as I did, Dizzy Gillespie at the Monterey Jazz Festival fill his cheeks with enough air to inflate a life-raft; Duke Ellington assuring everyone "I love you madly;" to hear Billie Holiday sing "God Bless the Child" (with narcs waiting by the door to take her to the slammer). And there was the night Bix died and someone came to Eddie's speakeasy to tell us the sad news, or when Louis Armstrong, in that Midwest city, had been cheered on stage but no first-class hotel would find him a room for the night.

Turning the pages of the sketchbooks, fingering the drawings, I feel near the old recalls of places and people. As a young journalist, New Orleans in the days of the sporting houses, the jailhouse and work songs of the chaingangs, all are here. Josephine Baker when the Charleston was new, one of my first sketches of her. Historic moments: hearing the first swing, the start of

## INTRODUCTION

While working on some of the histories I have produced on jazz music and its people, I have often felt the need for a dictionary in graphic form. For quick alphabetical information or renewing a contact with jazz figures or jazz terms. From Louis Armstrong under *A* to Zoot Suit under *Z*.

For many years, I put aside drawings and notes to be compiled later into such a graphic dictionary of jazz. John Huston, the film director, had helped me to pick out what we thought was best for the project, but then my interests were diverted and the portfolio disappeared. I thought I'd lost it between houses. Then one day, while hunting for some of my jazz graphics for the Smithsonian Institution in Washington, D.C., I came across a fat portfolio of drawings that had never been reproduced, the one I'd put together for the dictionary.

\*   \*   \*

Why a graphic dictionary of jazz personalities, jazz terms, special cities, dances, festivals, ways of playing? Aren't there good collections of photographs? Yes, but while I feel that photography can be art or journalism, it remains a seeker of surfaces, set to best capture in sunlight or under artificial brightness only what it can see in its lens, no matter how a master photographer can manipulate the result.

The graphic artist, be he Hogarth, Daumier, Norman Rockwell or Charles Schultz, adds the human quality, that matter of enigma which seeks a deeper truth or a more mortal atmosphere.

Since the mid-1920s, when as a teenage art student I began to fill sketchbooks with the jazz scene, to the

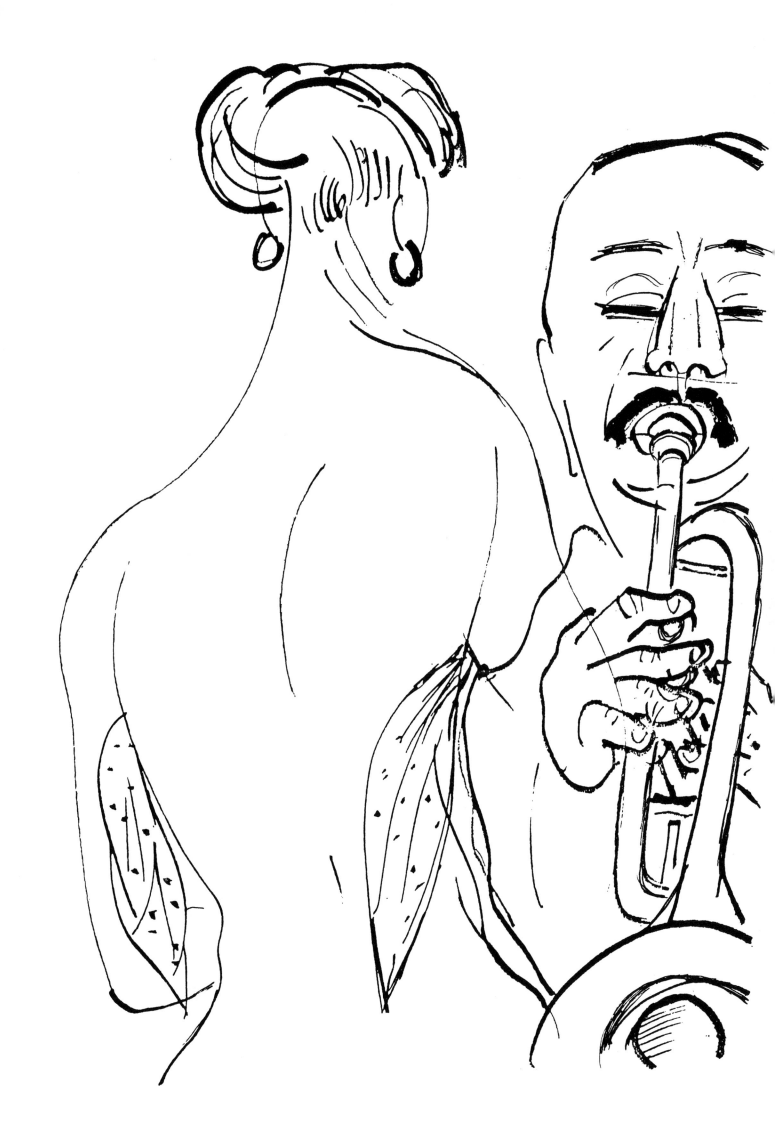

## CONTENTS

To two who really
had much to do with this book

Robert Wechsler
The best of editors

and

Ethel
Who is really co-author of this text:
hunter of data, titles, dates
and the true facts.

Much thanks for this shared gig!

And to Louis Armstrong, in memory of all
those talks we had on the set of *Hello Dolly.*

# JAZZ
## FROM A TO Z
## A GRAPHIC DICTIONARY

Drawings and Text by
## Stephen Longstreet

CATBIRD PRESS